Play Piano!

Alfred's Basic Adult Piano Course

Lesson · Theory · Sight Reading · Technic

An Easy Beginning Method for Busy Adults

WILLARD A. PALMER · MORTON MANUS · E. L. LANCASTER

Alfred

Foreword

Play Piano Now! Book 2 was designed for busy adults who want to learn to play quickly and easily. Students who have completed Book 1 know everything they need to continue their successful study of piano, using this book. In addition, adults who studied piano when they were younger and would now like to resume playing, will find this book helpful in reviewing and adding to their technique and musical knowledge.

Book 2 continues in the same style and pace as Book 1, gradually introducing music fundamentals followed by sufficient pages of reinforcement. Using favorite pieces and the popular conceptual core from *Alfred's Basic Adult Piano Course,* this all-new format allows students to progress steadily at a comfortable pace without having to repeat the same page again and again. The use of more pages on the same topic makes each practice session interesting and fresh, allowing for a thorough understanding of each subject before moving to something new.

Book 2 also continues its emphasis on one of the most important skills that adults must develop to insure long-term enjoyment of the piano—the ability to play at sight. Throughout the book are specially constructed *Sight Reading* exercises. Realizing that material can only be used for sight reading one time, the student should play these exercises only once each day. At the lesson, the student should play the exercise for the teacher without stopping, then discuss problems encountered during practice and at the lesson.

Also included in this new approach are *Technic* and *Write & Play* exercises, combined with appealing and familiar songs to perform. An added feature is specially marked exercises (*Writing* and *Rhythm*) that can be completed *Away from the Keyboard.*

Book 2 carefully prepares the student to understand the concept of keys while simultaneously developing the technique necessary for scale playing. Major keys introduced are C major, G major and F major; minor keys introduced are A minor, E minor and D minor—also included are the chromatic scale and $\frac{6}{8}$ time. The music that reinforces the keys is among the most beautiful ever written. The selections make the study of playing the piano the joy that is music—uplifting and inspiring.

The Glossary at the end of the book includes all the new terms and symbols used in Book 2, and the page(s) on which they are introduced. Also included are all the terms and symbols introduced in Book 1.

The authors wish you continued success in learning to play the piano. Whether you perform for your own enjoyment or for a party of friends, you'll find that playing the piano is a gift you can give yourself that lasts for a lifetime!

Willard A. Palmer • **Morton Manus** • **E. L. Lancaster**

Table of Contents

Unit 1

The Natural Sign, Half Steps and Whole Steps

Natural Sign ♮

Cancels a sharp (♯) or flat (♭).

When a natural (♮) appears before a note, it applies to that note for the rest of the measure!

On with the Show!

Notes played between the main beats of the measure and held across the beat are called **syncopated notes.**

Syncopated note

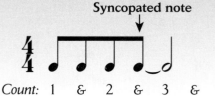

Count: 1 & 2 & 3 & 4 &

March tempo

f

On with the show!   Strike up the band!   Come on, let's go!

8

Give them a hand! Bring on the clowns, tum-blers and bears!

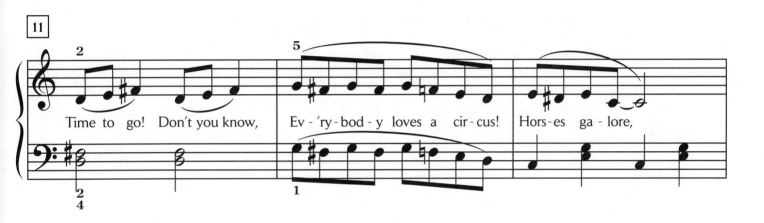

11

Time to go! Don't you know, Ev - 'ry-bod - y loves a cir-cus! Hors-es ga - lore,

14

See how they prance! What's e-ven more, El-e-phants dance! On with the show!

18

On with the show! Ev - 'ry-bod - y loves it when the cir-cus comes to town!

Half Steps

A **half step** is the distance from any key to the very next key up or down, black or white, *with no key between.*

The sharp sign ♯ raises a note a half step.

The flat sign ♭ lowers a note a half step.

Each black key may be named two ways, as shown.

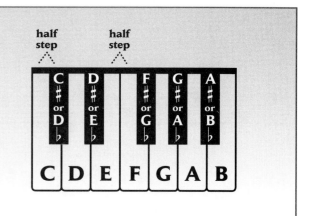

Remember: The natural sign ♮ is used to cancel a sharp or a flat. (A note after a natural is always a white key!)

Practice Exercise: Sight Reading

Every musician must learn to read and play at sight (the first time the music is performed). Follow the practice directions, working to play each example perfectly the first time.

1. Clap (or tap) RH and count aloud; clap (or tap) LH and count aloud.

2. Play RH and count aloud; play LH and count aloud.

3. Play hands together. and count aloud.

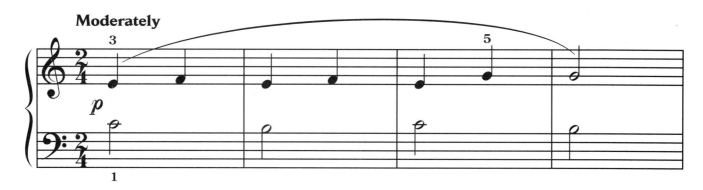

Whole Steps

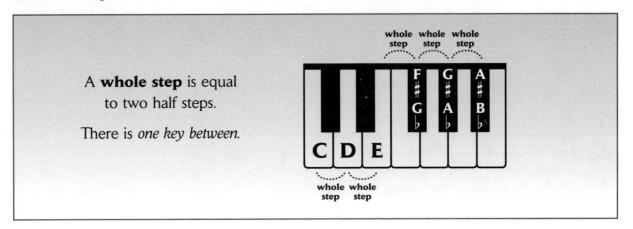

A **whole step** is equal
to two half steps.

There is *one key between*.

Remember: When a sharp or flat appears before a
note, it applies to that note each time it is used in the
rest of the measure, unless it is cancelled by a natural.

Practice Exercise: Sight Reading

1.   Clap (or tap) & count.

2.   Play & count.

3.   Play & sing (or say) the note names.

Lively

* A sharp or flat continues when a note is tied to the following measure.
  It is not necessary to re-write the sharp or flat before the second of the two tied notes.

Written Exercise: Away from the Keyboard

1. Write a half note *up* from the given note to make a *half step*. Add a flat or a natural if indicated in the square below. Turn the stems *up* in the treble clef, *down* in the bass clef.

2. Write the name of each note in the square below it.

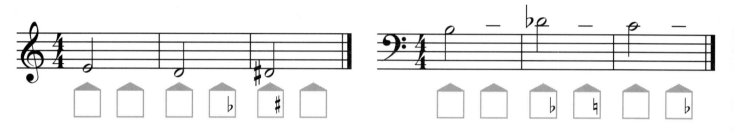

3. Write a half note *down* from the given note to make a *half step*. Add a sharp or natural if indicated in the square below. Turn the stems *up* in the treble clef, *down* in the bass clef.

4. Write the name of each note in the square below it.

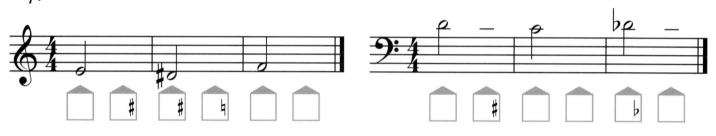

5. Write a half note *up* from the given note to make a *whole step*. Add a sharp or a flat if indicated in the square below. Turn the stems *up* in the treble clef, *down* in the bass clef.

6. Write the name of each note in the square below it.

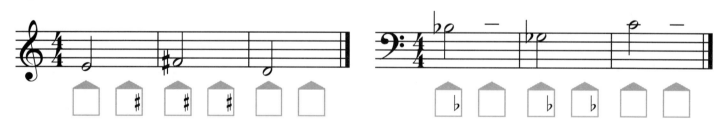

7. Write a half note *down* from the given note to make a *whole step*. Add a sharp or a flat if indicated in the square below. Turn the stems *up* in the treble clef, *down* in the bass clef.

8. Write the name of each note in the square below it.

The Song That Never Ends!

If you feel that you must end this song, do not stop at the last measure! Repeat the
first four measures, gradually fading away and ending with the first chord of measure 5.

*The eighth notes may be played a bit unevenly:

long   short   long   short, *etc.*

Unit 2

Tetrachords, The Major Scale, Triads

Tetrachords

A **tetrachord** is a series of four notes having a pattern of *whole step, whole step, half step.*

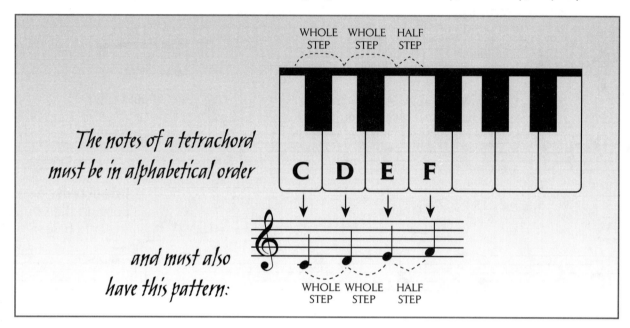

Play the following tetrachords. Finger the LH tetrachords 5 4 3 2; RH 2 3 4 5.

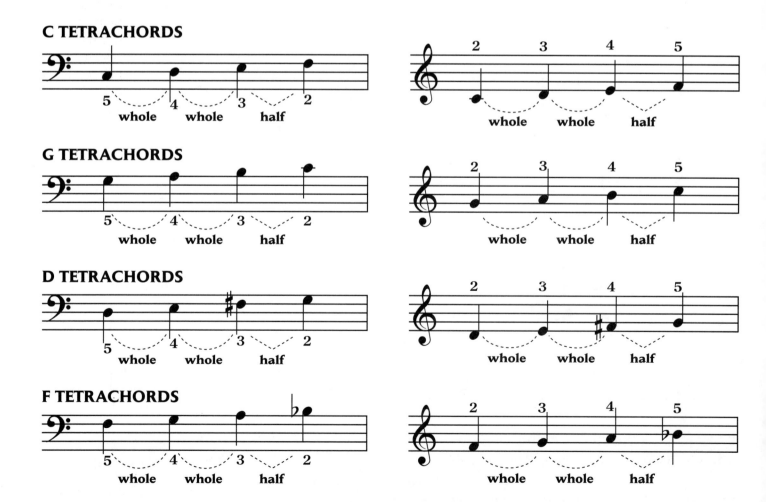

C TETRACHORDS

5   4   3   2
whole   whole   half

2   3   4   5
whole   whole   half

G TETRACHORDS

5   4   3   2
whole   whole   half

2   3   4   5
whole   whole   half

D TETRACHORDS

5   4   3   2
whole   whole   half

2   3   4   5
whole   whole   half

F TETRACHORDS

5   4   3   2
whole   whole   half

2   3   4   5
whole   whole   half

The Major Scale

The **major scale** is made of *two tetrachords* joined by a *whole step*.
The second tetrachord of the C major scale begins on G.

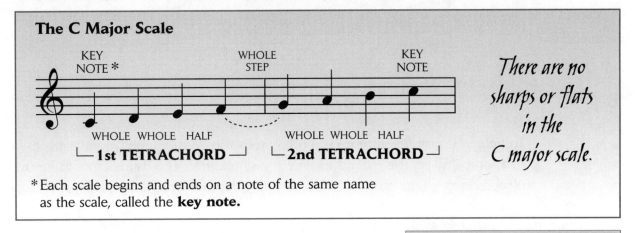

* Each scale begins and ends on a note of the same name
  as the scale, called the **key note.**

Technic Exercise: Preparation for Scale Playing

Important: Since there are 8 notes in the C major scale and we only have 5 fingers, this technique must be mastered: *passing the thumb under the 3rd finger, and crossing the 3rd finger over the thumb!* This exercise will make it easy.

Play hands separately. Begin very slowly.
Keep the wrist loose and quiet!

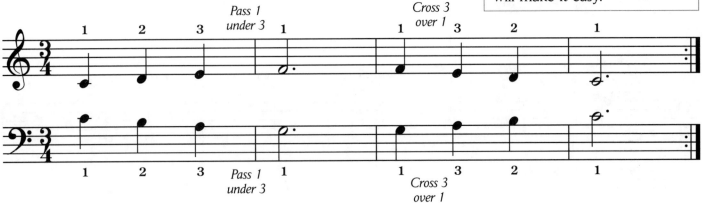

Playing the C Major Scale

As soon as the thumb has played the first note (while the 2nd finger is playing the second note), pass the thumb under to the base of the 4th finger, so it will be ready to play its next note in advance. This is one of the most important secrets of smooth, legato scale playing!

Moderately slow

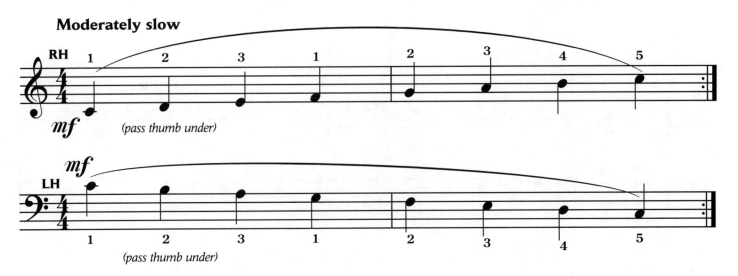

Simile

Continue in the same manner.

Technic Exercise: Thumb-Under

To help you play scales more smoothly, start the thumb-under motion just as you play the harmonic 2nd on the second beat of each measure. The thumb should be over the key played on the third beat well in advance. Keep the wrist loose and quiet. *Lift off* on the fourth count.

Moderately slow to moderately fast

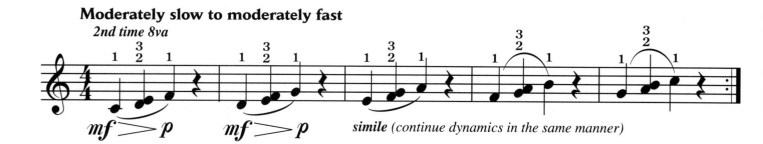

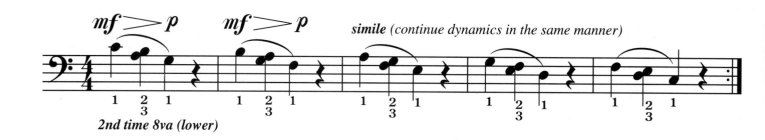

Playing the C Major Scale—Ascending and Descending

Practice the C major scale hands separately. Begin **slowly** and gradually increase speed. *Lean* the hand slightly in the direction you are moving. The hand should move smoothly along, with no twisting motion of the wrist!

New Dynamic Sign

$\textbf{\textit{ff}}$ *(fortissimo)* = very loud

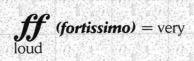

Joy to the World

Handel is well-known for his oratorio
Messiah, which is performed
throughout the Christmas season.

George Frideric Handel
(1685–1759)

*Scales occur often in melodies. This favorite melody is made up almost entirely of the C major scale.

Write and Play Exercise

1. In the treble staff under the squares, write the notes of the C major scale. Use whole notes. Add fingering above the notes and then play.

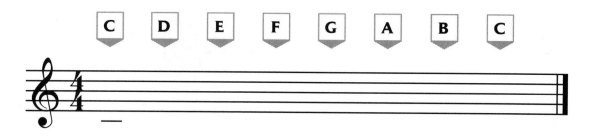

2. In the bass staff over the squares, write the notes of the C major scale. Use whole notes. Add fingering below the notes and then play.

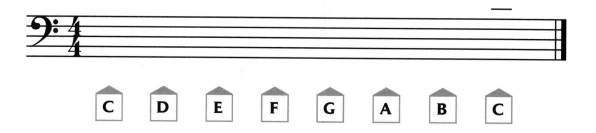

3. Write the name of each note in the square below it—then play and say the note names.

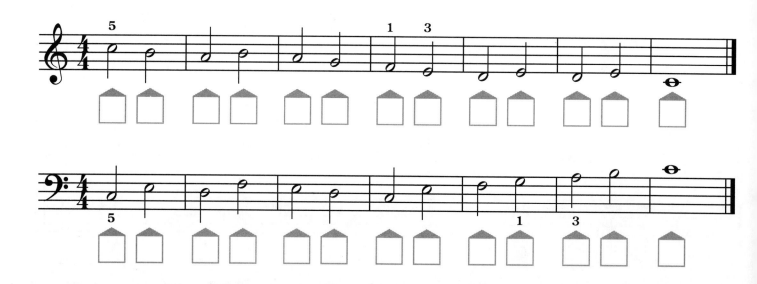

Practice Exercise: Sight Reading

1.

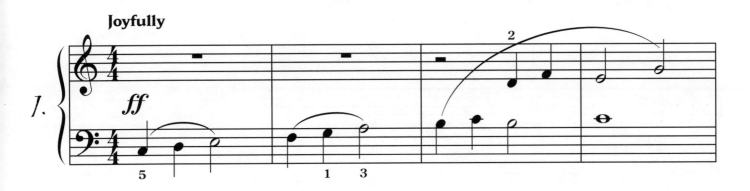

5.

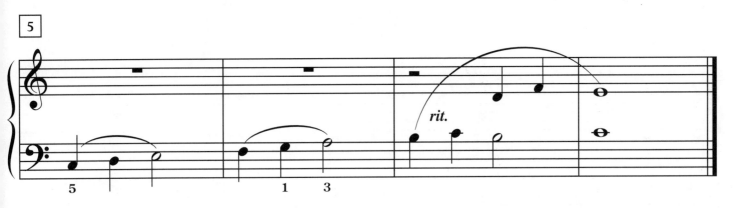

2.

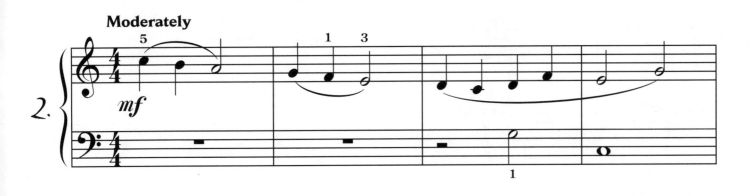

5.

Take Me Out to the Ball Game

Find the C major scale in the right hand.

Words by Jack Norworth
Music by Albert von Tilzer

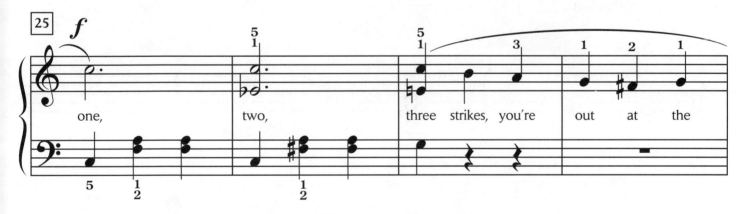

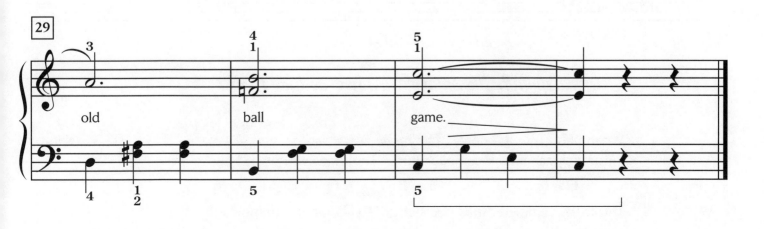

Triads

A **triad** is a three-note chord.

The three notes of a triad are the **root,** the **third,** and the **fifth.**

FIFTH (5) ——— 5th from
THIRD (3) ——— 3rd from
ROOT (1) ——— ROOT

The root is the note on which the triad is built and from which the triad gets its name. The root of a C triad is C.

Triads in **root position**   LINE ——— 5th
(with root at the bottom)   LINE ——— 3rd
always look like this: LINE ——— ROOT

or this: SPACE ——— 5th
SPACE ——— 3rd
SPACE ——— ROOT

Triads may be built on any note of any scale.

Triads Built on the C Major Scale

Play with RH:

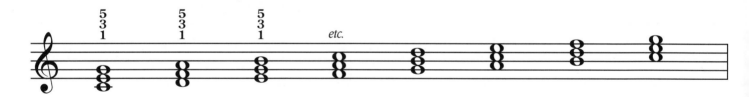

5
3
1   etc.

Play with LH:

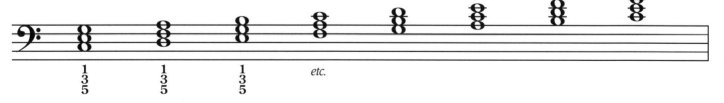

1
3
5   etc.

Listen carefully to the sound of these root-position triads!

When you name the notes of any *triad in root position,* you will always skip *one* letter of the musical alphabet between each note. The triads you played above are:

    C E G   **D** F A   **E** G B   **F** A C   **G** B D   **A** C E   **B** D F

This is the complete "triad vocabulary." It should be memorized!

Cockles and Mussels

Key and Key Signature

Music based on any particular scale is said to be in the **key** of that scale. If there are sharps or flats in the scale, they are shown at the beginning of each staff. This is called the **key signature.**

Irish Folk Song

Key of C Major
Key Signature: no ♯, no ♭

Moderately slow

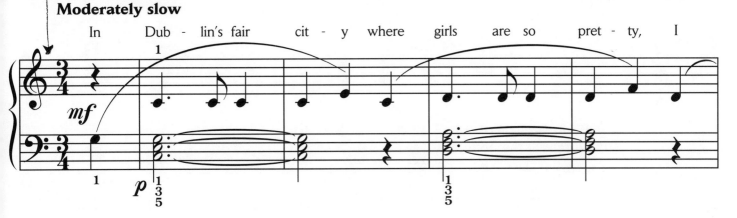

In Dub - lin's fair cit - y where girls are so pret - ty, I

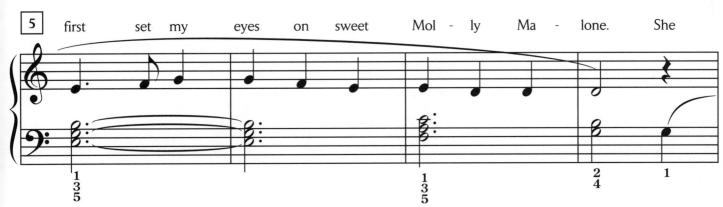

first set my eyes on sweet Mol - ly Ma - lone. She

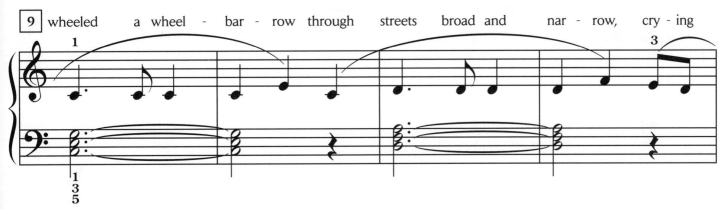

wheeled a wheel - bar - row through streets broad and nar - row, cry - ing

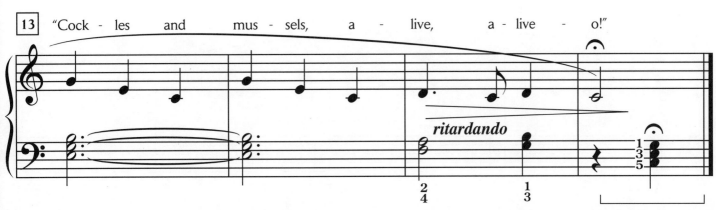

"Cock - les and mus - sels, a - live, a - live - o!"

ritardando

When reading triads in root position, keep your eyes on the lowest note rather than trying to read all three notes.

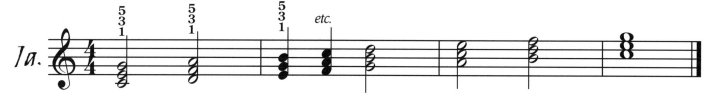

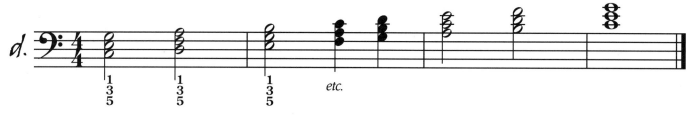

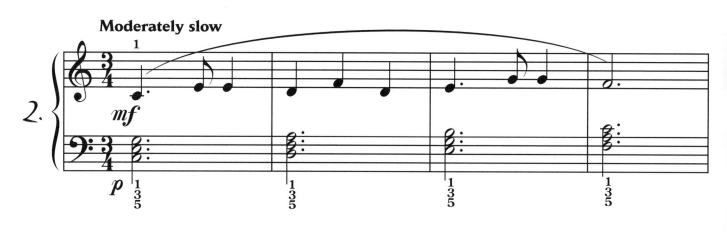

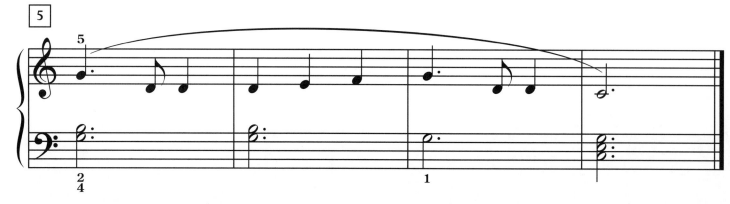

Unit 2 **23**
Tetrachords, The Major Scale, Triads

Written Exercise: Away from the Keyboard

1. Circle the triad on the bass staff that matches the letter name of its root in the middle column.

2. Circle the triad on the treble staff that matches the letter name of its root in the middle column.

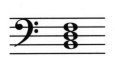
 A

 B

 C

 D

 E

 F

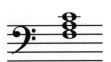 G

Unit 3

Primary Chords in C Major, Extended Positions

Primary Chords in C Major

The three most important chords in any key are those built on the 1st, 4th and 5th notes of the scale. These are called the **primary chords** of the key.

The chords are identified by the Roman numerals **I, IV** and **V** (1, 4 and 5).
The **V** chord usually adds the note a 7th above the root to make a **V⁷** (say "5-7") chord.

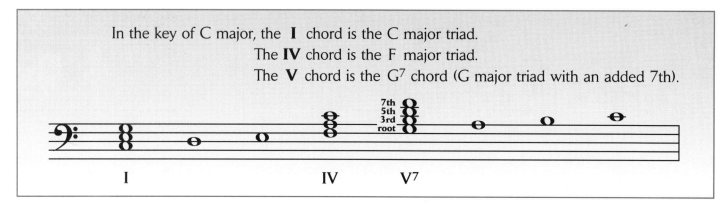

Chord Progressions

When we change from one chord to another, we call this a **chord progression.**

When all chords are in root position, the hand must leap from one chord to the next. To make the chord progressions easier to play and sound better, the **IV** and **V⁷** chords may be played in other positions by moving one or more of the higher chord tones down an octave.

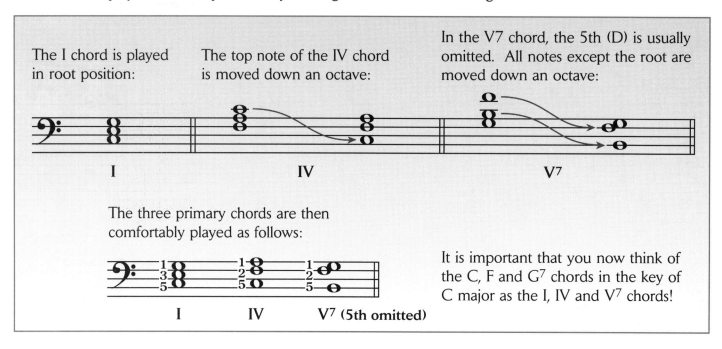

Play the following line several times, saying the numerals of each chord as you play.

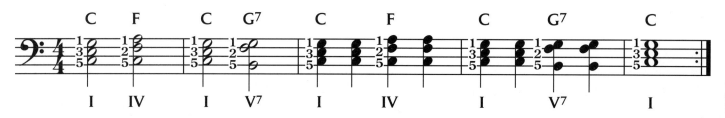

About the Blues

Music called **blues** has long been a part of the American musical heritage. We find it in the music of many popular songwriters, in ballads, boogie, and rock.

Blues music follows a basic formula, that is, a standard chord progression. If you learn the formula for *Got Those Blues!* you will be able to play the blues in any key you learn, simply by applying the formula to that key.

Formula for the Blues

There are 12 measures in one chorus of the blues:

4 measures of the **I** chord
2 measures of the **IV** chord
2 measures of the **I** chord
1 measure of the **V⁷** chord
1 measure of the **IV** chord
2 measures of the **I** chord

*The eighth notes may be played a bit unevenly:

long   short long   short, *etc.*

The C Major Blues Progression

Remember: The blues progression is a series of chords that uses the **I, IV, V^7** chords and is generally 12 measures long.

The C Major Blues Progression

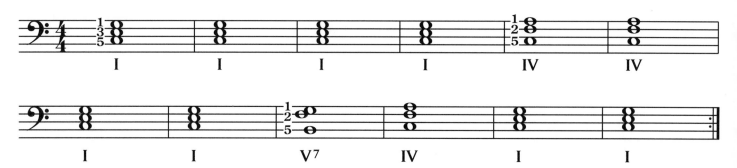

Carefree Boogie uses the blues progression two times. The first twelve measures use block chords. Notice that measure 12 has been changed from a I chord to a V^7 chord so that the blues progression can be repeated. When the progression is repeated beginning in measure 13, three-note chords are not used but the bass line uses single notes from these chords. The last six measures are an added ending.

Gayle Kowalchyk
E. L. Lancaster

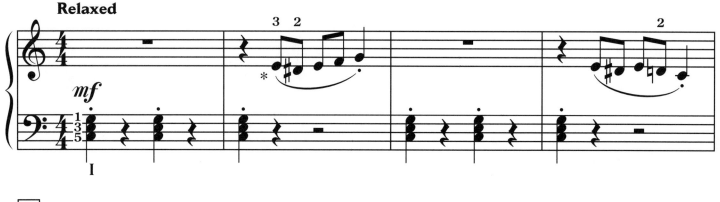

*Eighth notes may be played unevenly, in long-short pairs.

"Carefree Boogie" from BOOGIE 'N' BLUES, Book 2, by Gayle Kowalchyk and E. L. Lancaster
Copyright © MCMXCIII by Alfred Publishing Co., Inc.

Written Exercise: Away from the Keyboard

1. Circle the 1st, 4th and 5th notes of each of the scales below.
These notes are the roots of the primary triads.

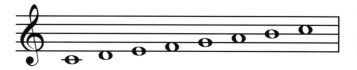

2. In the squares above the staff, write the names of the notes in each chord.

3. On the staff, circle the root of each chord.

4. On the line below the staff, write the name of the chord (**I, IV** or **V⁷**).

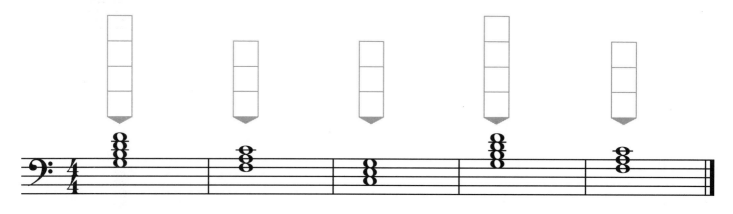

To make the chord progressions easier to play and sound better, the **IV** and **V⁷** chords may be played in other positions by moving one or more of the higher chord tones down an octave. In the **V⁷** chord, the 5th is usually omitted.

5. In the squares above the staff, write the names of the notes in each chord.

6. On the staff, circle the root of each chord.

7. On the line below the staff, write the name of the chord (**I, IV** or **V⁷**).

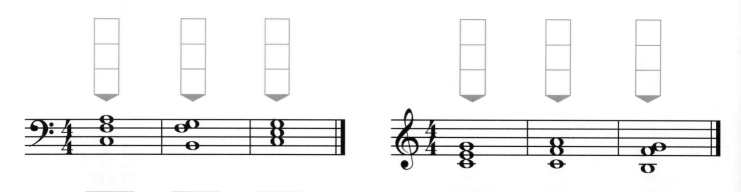

Practice Exercise: Sight Reading

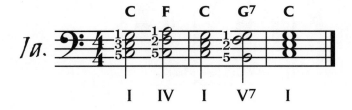

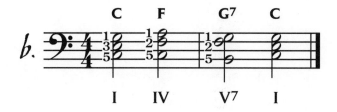

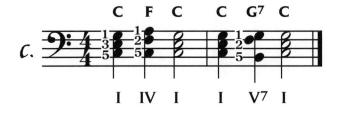

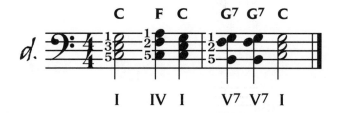

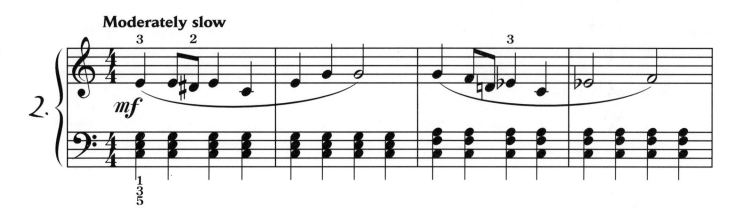

Eighth notes may be played in long-short pairs.

RH: An Extended Position

On Top of Old Smoky begins and ends with the RH in an **extended position.**

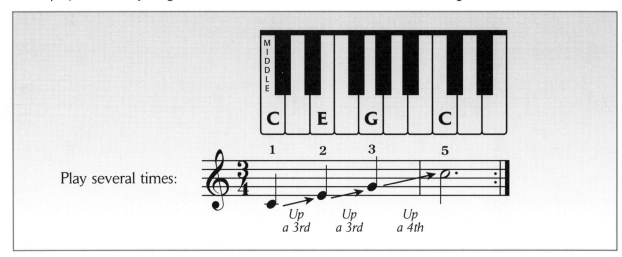

Play several times:

Up a 3rd *Up a 3rd* *Up a 4th*

LH Review: Block Chords and Broken Chords in C Major

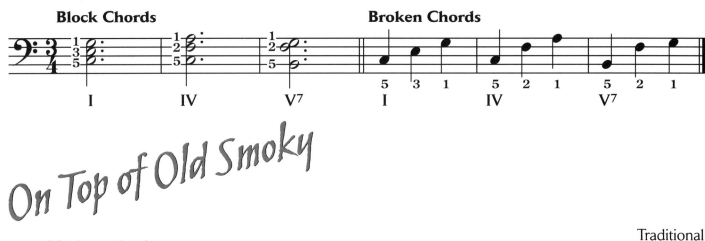

Block Chords **Broken Chords**

I   IV   V⁷   I   IV   V⁷

On Top of Old Smoky

Traditional

Moderately slow

Extended position

mf On top of old Smok - y,   All cov-er'd with

snow,   I lost my true lov -

er, From a - court - in' too slow. For

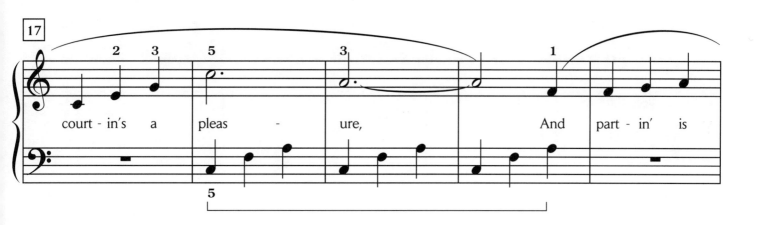

court - in's a pleas - ure, And part - in' is

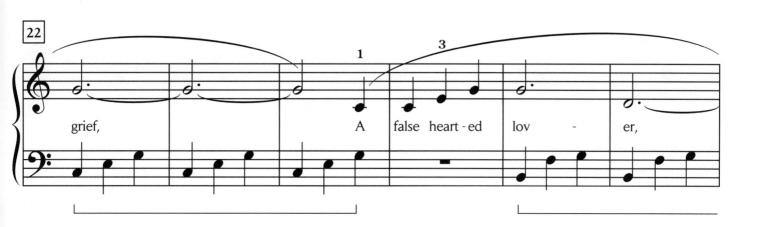

grief, A false heart - ed lov - er,

Is worse than a thief. *rit.*

Written Exercise: Away from the Keyboard

Draw a line from each set of notes to its matching word in the middle column.

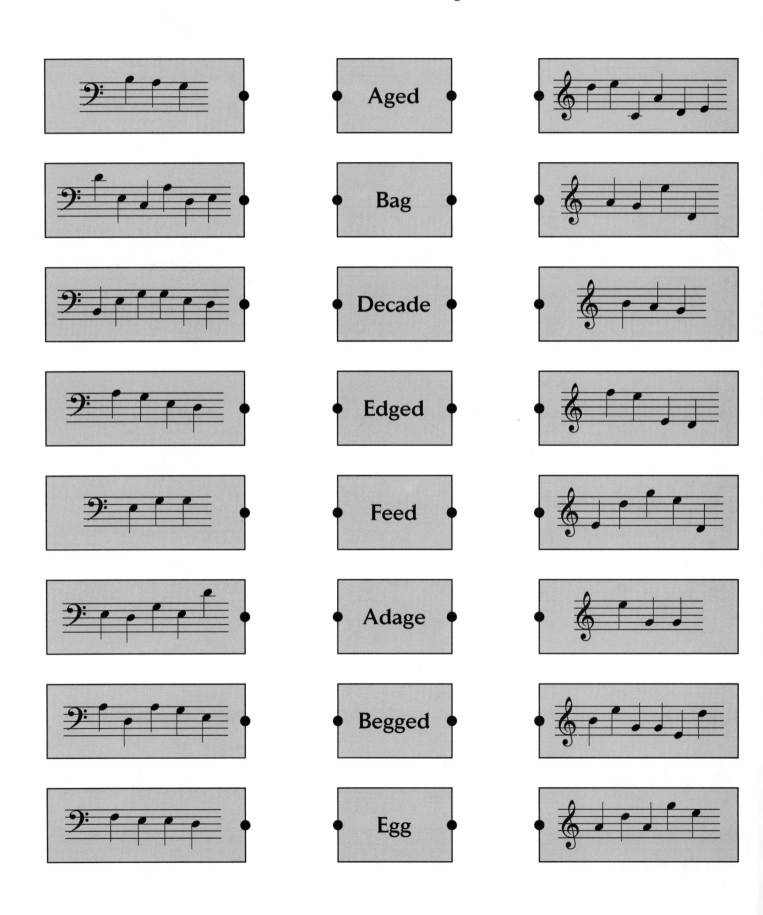

Practice Exercise: Sight Reading

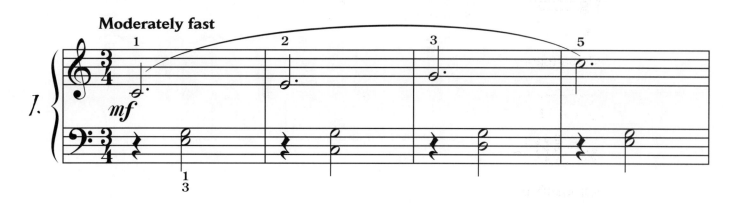

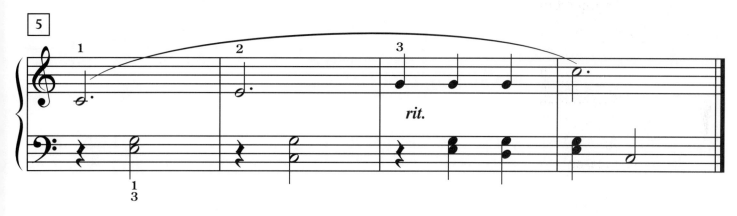

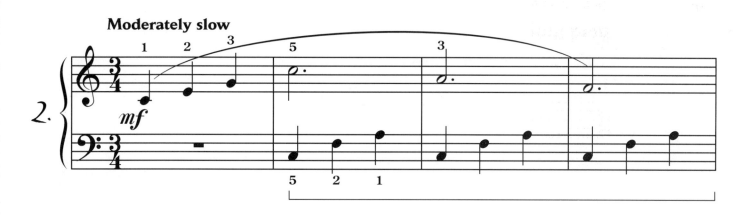

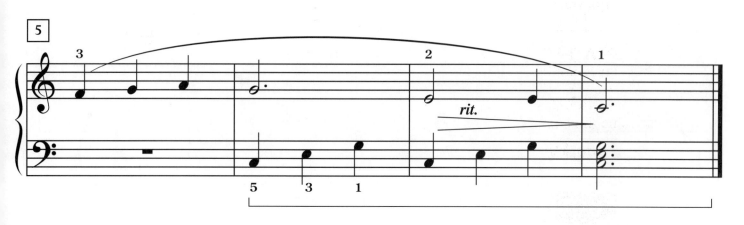

RH: Another Extended Position

Down in the Valley uses a RH extended position beginning on G and ends with
a LH extended position beginning on C.

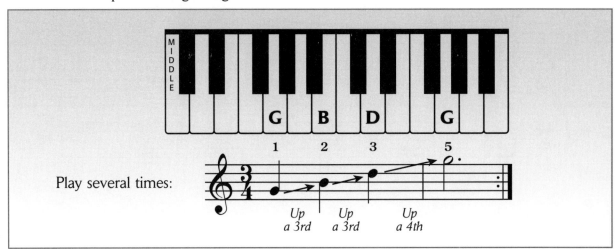

LH Review: Broken Chords in C Major

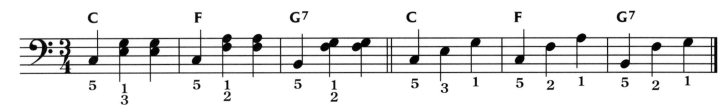

Down in the Valley

American Folk Song

Moderately

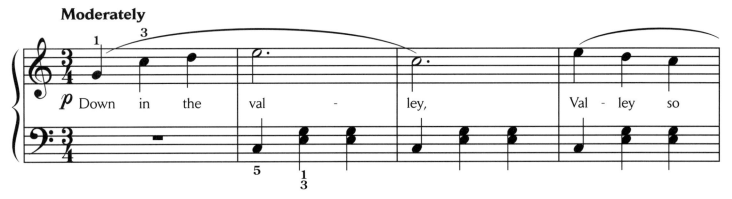

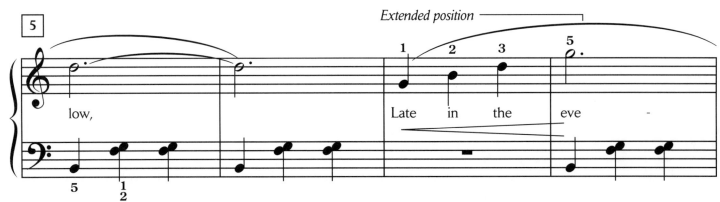

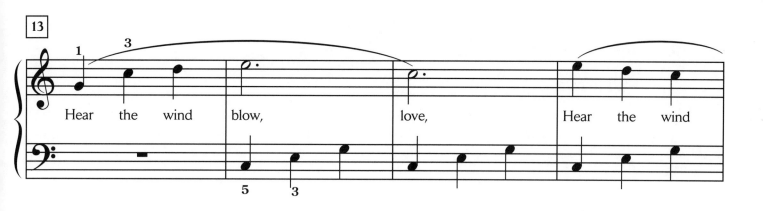

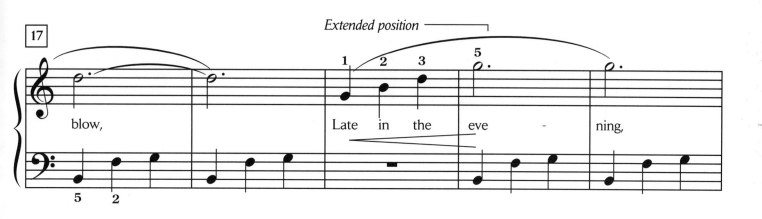

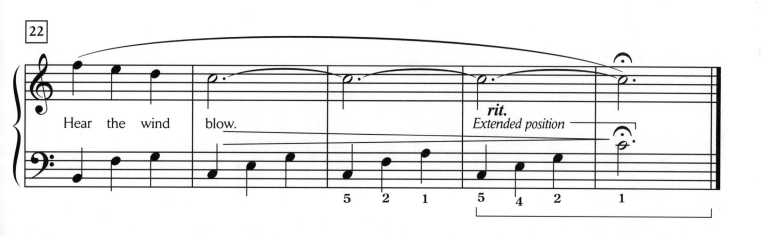

Write and Play Exercise: LH Extended Positions

Each of the following lines is played with a LH extended position beginning on a different note.

1. Write the names of the notes in the boxes.

2. Play, using the damper pedal as indicated.

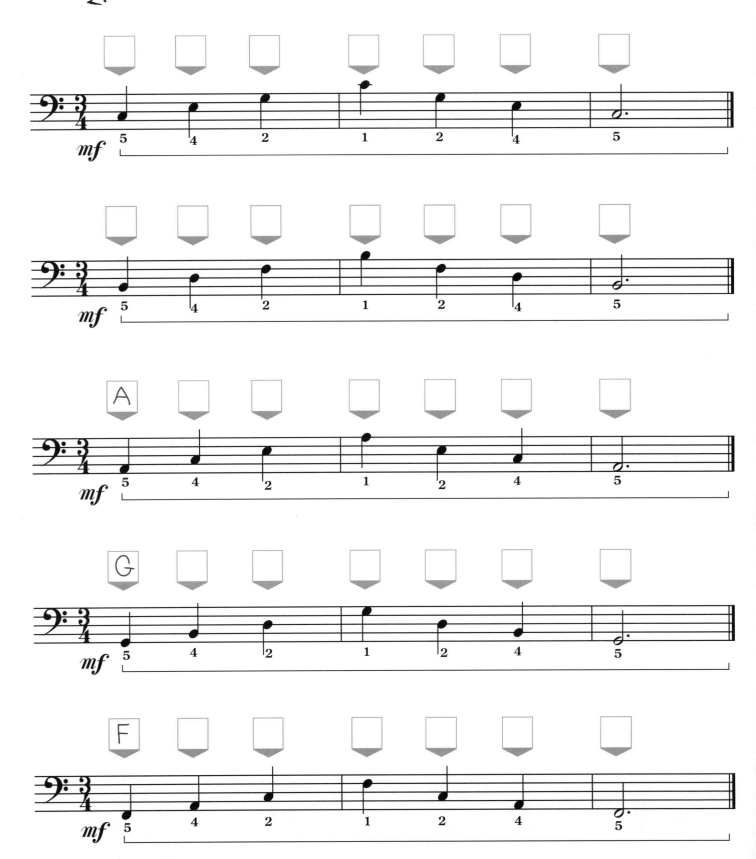

Write and Play Exercise: RH Extended Positions

Each of the following lines is played with a RH extended position beginning on a different note.

1. Write the names of the notes in the boxes.

2. Play, using the damper pedal as indicated.

RH: A New Extended Position

Bridal Chorus uses a new RH extended position beginning on G.

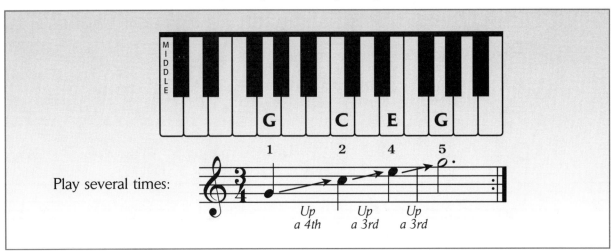

Play several times:

*Up
a 4th*   *Up
a 3rd*   *Up
a 3rd*

Bridal Chorus
from "Lohengrin"

This famous chorus from Wagner's opera Lohengrin
*is the music used by many brides as they enter the
wedding chapel. The first performance of this opera
was conducted by Liszt in 1850.*

Richard Wagner
(1813–1883)

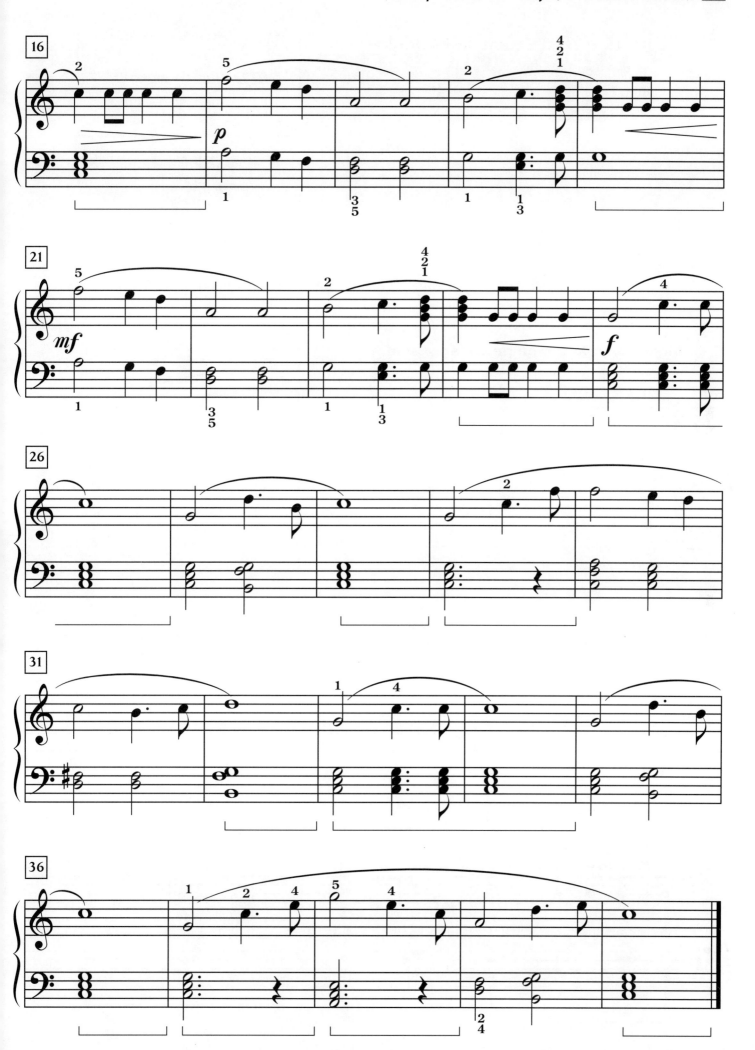

New Dynamic Sign

mp *(mezzo piano)* =
moderately soft

a tempo means
resume original speed

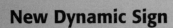

Far Beyond My Imagination

Find the C major scale in the right hand.

Moderately slow, with much expression

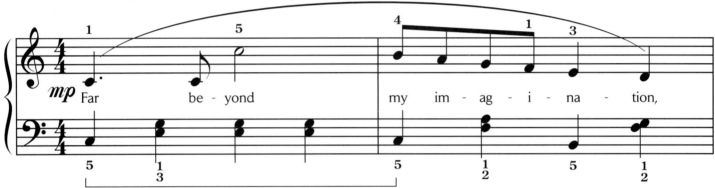

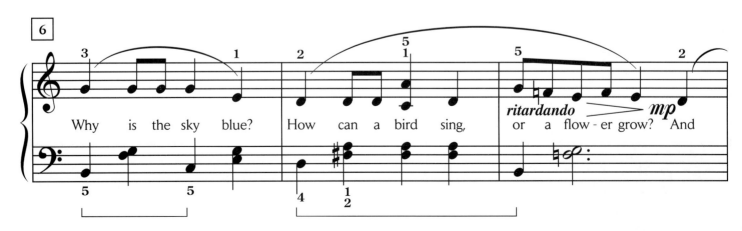

far be-yond all my un-der-stand - ing, I be-lieve

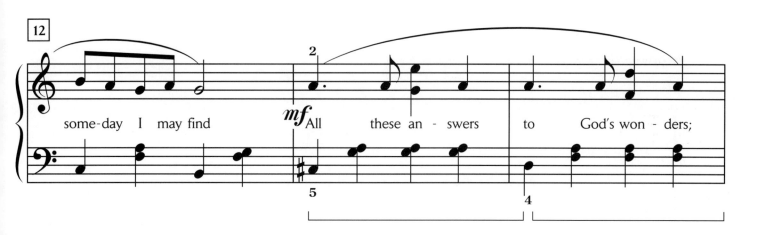

some-day I may find *mf* All these an - swers to God's won - ders;

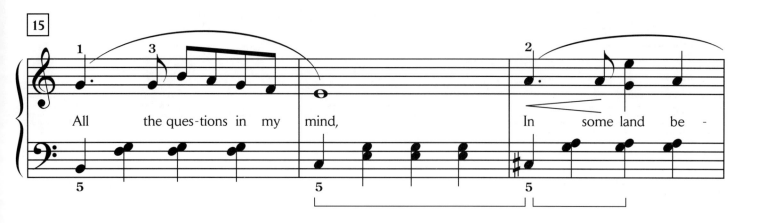

All the ques-tions in my mind, In some land be -

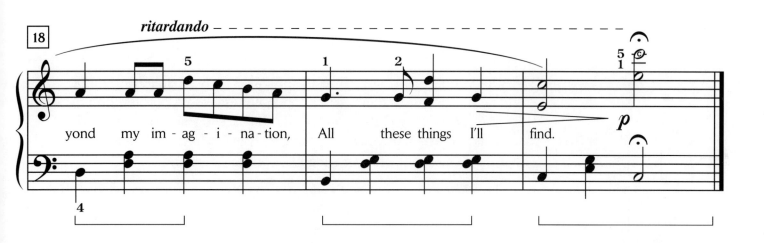

ritardando

yond my im-ag-i-na-tion, All these things I'll find.

Unit 4

The Key of G Major

The G Major Scale

Remember that the major scale is made of two tetrachords *joined* by a whole step. The second tetrachord of the G major scale begins on D.

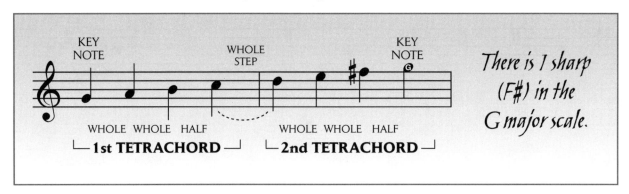

The Key of G Major

A piece based on the G major scale is in the **key of G major.** Since F is *sharp* in the G scale, every F will be sharp in the key of G major.

Instead of placing a sharp before every F in the entire piece, the sharp is indicated at the beginning in the *key signature.*

Key of G Major
Key Signature: 1 sharp (F♯)
Play all F's sharp throughout.

Practice the G major scale *hands separately.* Begin *slowly* and gradually increase speed. Keep the wrist loose and quiet.

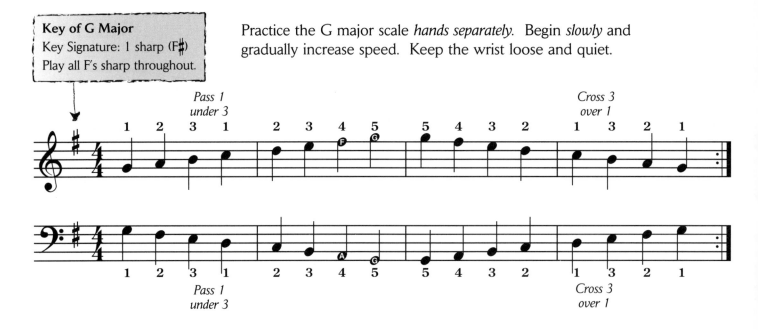

Important! After you have learned the G major scale hands separately, you may play the hands together. When the scale is played as written on the staffs above, the LH descends as the RH ascends, and vice versa. This is called **contrary motion**—both hands play the *same numbered* fingers at the same time, while moving in opposite directions!

You may also play the C major scale at the bottom of page 14 with the hands together, in *contrary motion.*

Plaisir d'Amour

Giovanni Martini
(1706–1784)

Key of G Major
Key Signature: 1 sharp (F♯)
Play all F's sharp throughout.

Martini, an Italian, is known as a teacher, writer and composer. "Plaisir d'Amour," one of his most famous compositions, was made into a popular song by Elvis Presley.

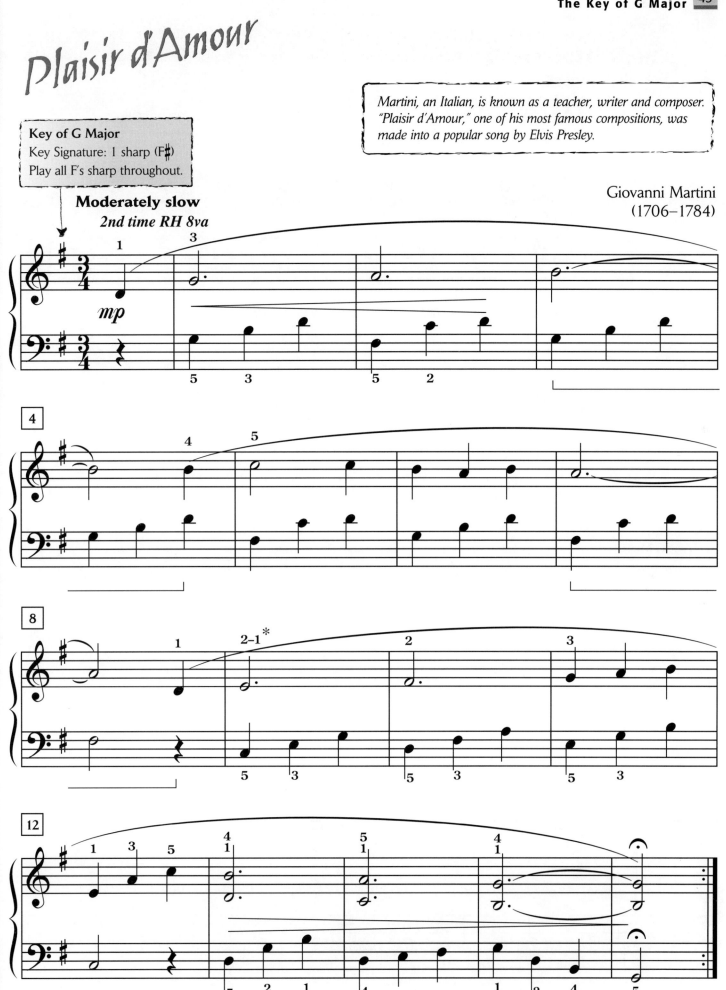

*Finger substitution: While holding the note down with finger 2, change to finger 1 on the 2nd beat.

Write and Play Exercise

1. In the treble staff under the squares, write the notes of the G major scale.
Use whole notes. Add fingering above the notes and then play.

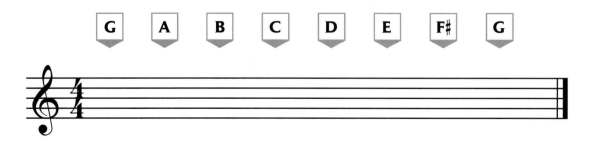

2. In the bass staff over the squares, write the notes of the G major scale.
Use whole notes. Add fingering below the notes and then play.

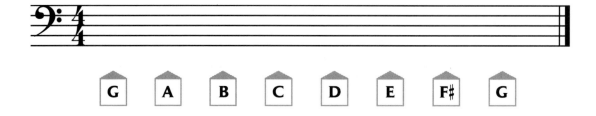

3. Write the name of each note in the square below it—then play and say the note names.

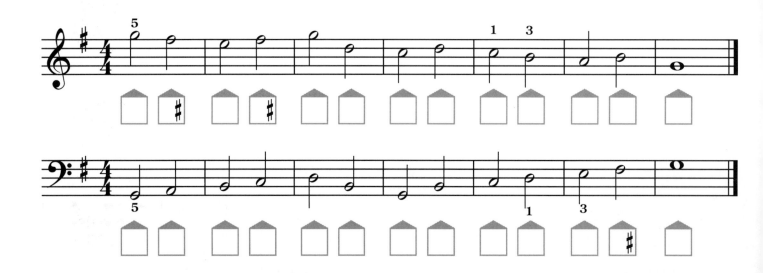

Primary Chords in G Major

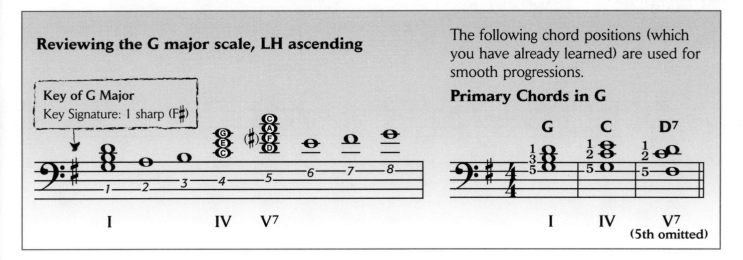

Reviewing the G major scale, LH ascending

Key of G Major
Key Signature: 1 sharp (F♯)

The following chord positions (which you have already learned) are used for smooth progressions.

Primary Chords in G

Play this chord progression several times, saying the chord names and numerals aloud:

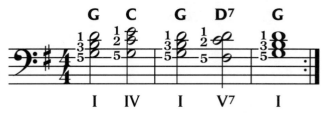

The Marines' Hymn

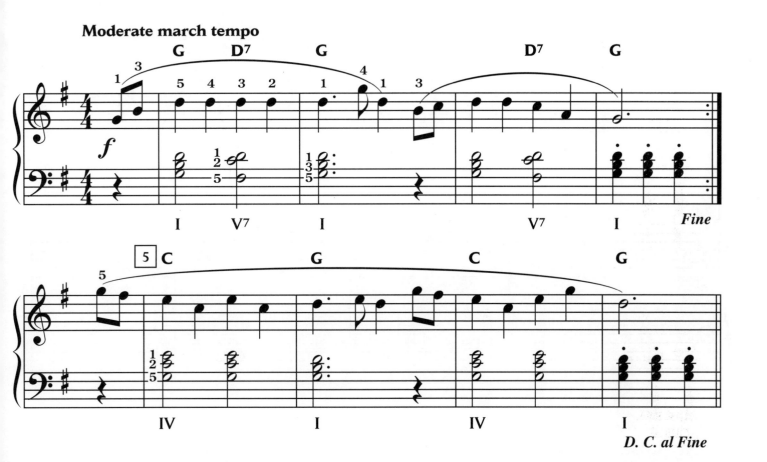

Moderate march tempo

D. C. al Fine

Practice Exercise: Sight Reading

1a.

b.

c.

d.

2.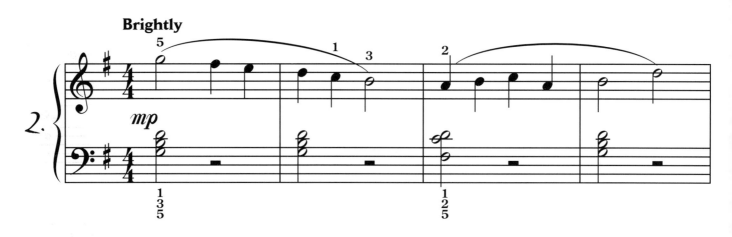

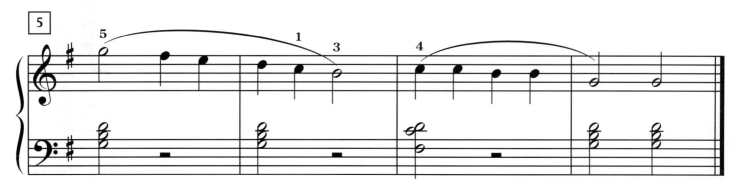

Why Am I Blue?

1st and 2nd endings

1. *(Play 1st time only!)*   2. *(Play 2nd time)*

Moderately slow blues tempo

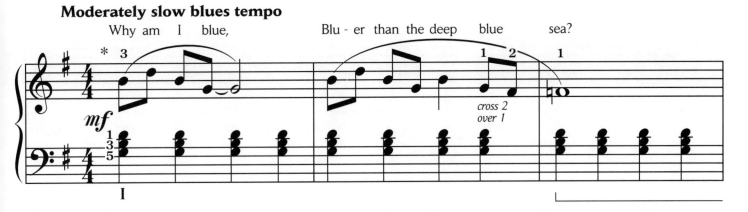

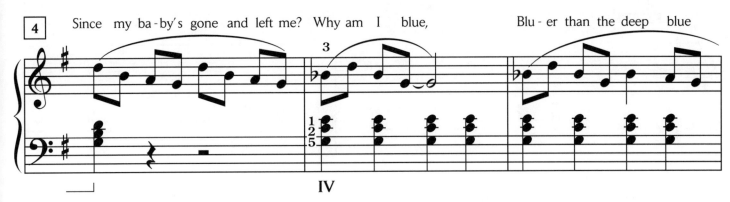

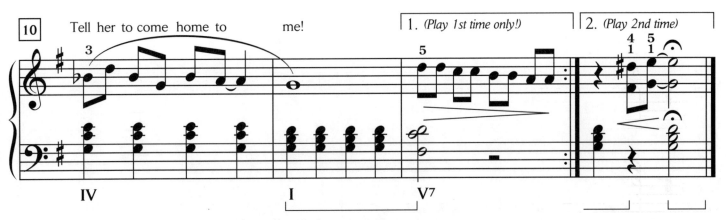

Important! Compare the Roman numerals in this piece with those
in *Got Those Blues!* on page 25.

*Eighth notes may be played unevenly, in long-short pairs.

Technic Exercise: Changing Fingers on the Same Note

Sometimes it is necessary to replay the same note with a different finger.
Practice the following line to prepare for *The Can-Can*.

The Can-Can

The lively, carefree and flowing melody of "The Can-Can" is typical of music that Offenbach used in his many operettas. The works of this famous French composer have been performed throughout the world.

Jacques Offenbach
(1819–1880)

*Descending G major scale

Written Exercise: Away from the Keyboard

1. In the squares above the staff, write the names of the notes in each chord.

2. On the staff, circle the root of each chord.

3. On the line below the staff, write the name of the chord (**I, IV** or **V⁷**).

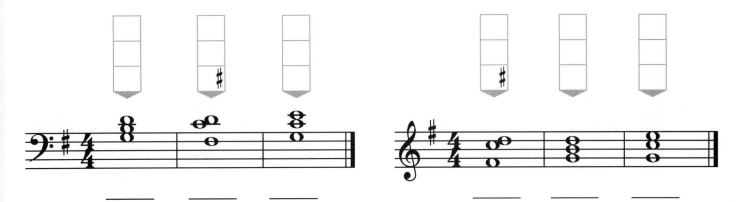

_____   _____   _____   _____   _____   _____

4. Draw a line from each box to its matching box in the adjacent column(s).

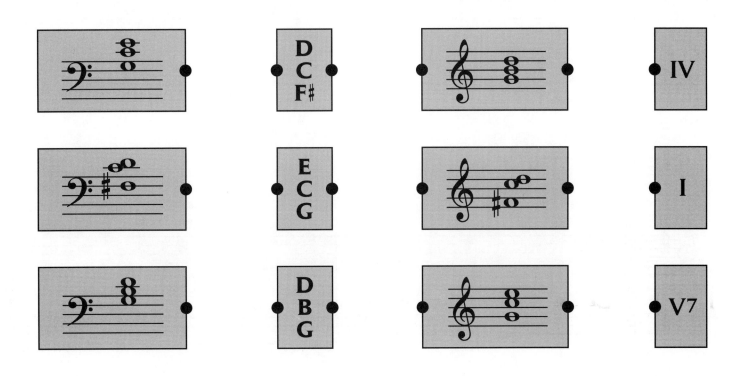

Practice Exercise: Sight Reading

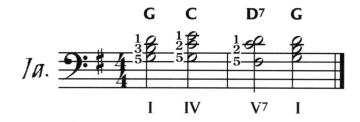

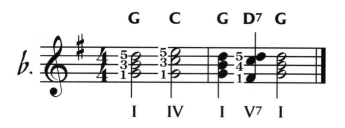

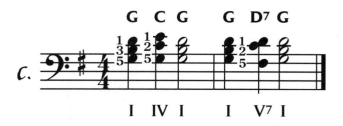

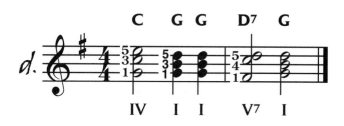

Moderately slow blues tempo

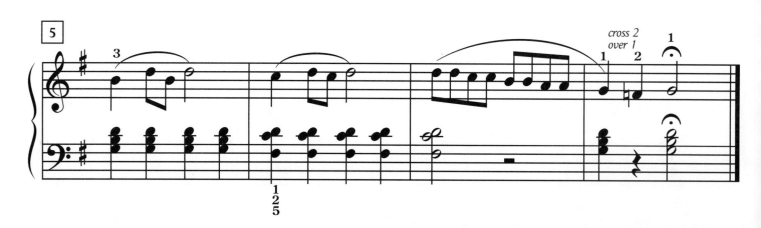

New Dynamic Sign

pp **(pianissimo)** = very soft

The Streets of Laredo

American Folk Song

Liebestraum
(Theme from No. 3)

D. S. 𝄋 al Fine

D. S. 𝄋 al Fine (Dal Segno al Fine) means *repeat from the sign 𝄋 and play to the end (**Fine**).*

Franz Liszt
(1811–1886)

Moderately, with feeling

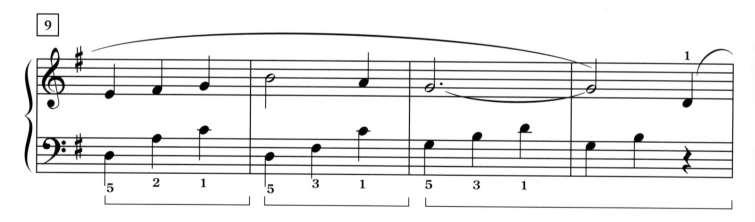

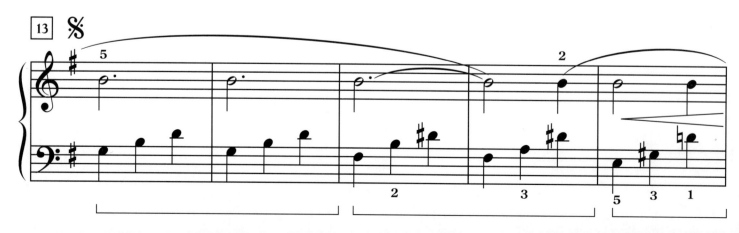

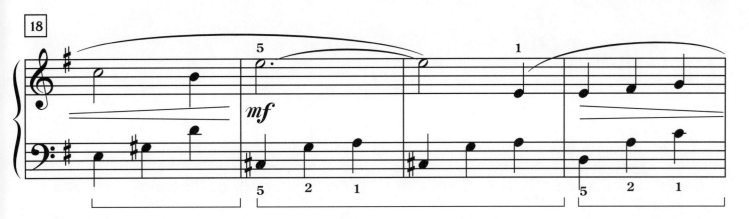

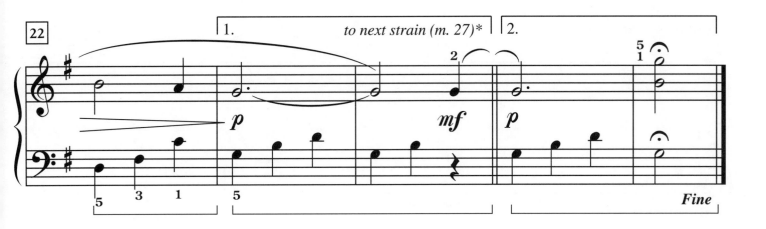

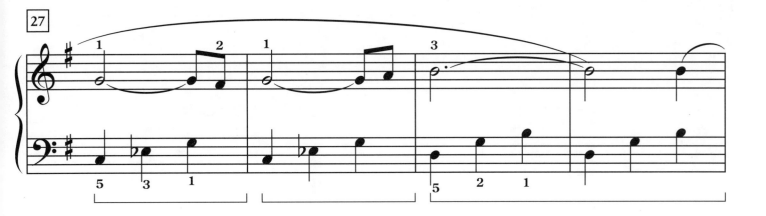

D. S. ℅ al Fine

* Do not repeat. After playing the first ending, go to measure 27.

** **poco** = little. In this case, it means a little *ritardando*.

La Cucaracha

Traditional

*Play the C and D together, with the side of the thumb.

Unit 5

The Key of F Major

The F Major Scale

Remember that the major scale is made of two tetrachords *joined* by a whole step. The second tetrachord of the F major scale begins on C.

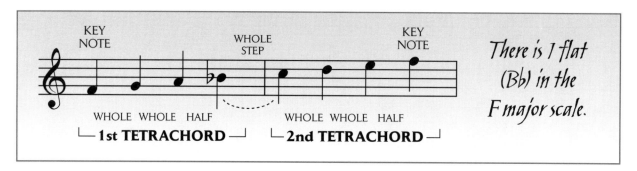

There is 1 flat (B♭) in the F major scale.

The Key of F Major

A piece based on the F major scale is in the **key of F major.** Since B is *flat* in the F scale, every B will be flat in the key of F major.

Instead of placing a flat before every B in the entire piece, the flat is indicated at the beginning in the *key signature.*

Practice the F major scale hands separately. Begin slowly and gradually increase speed. Keep the wrist loose and quiet.

Key of F Major
Key Signature: 1 flat (B♭)
Play all B's flat throughout.

To play the F major scale with the RH, the 5th finger is not used!
The fingers fall in the following groups: 1 2 3 4 – 1 2 3 4 ascending;
4 3 2 1 – 4 3 2 1 descending.

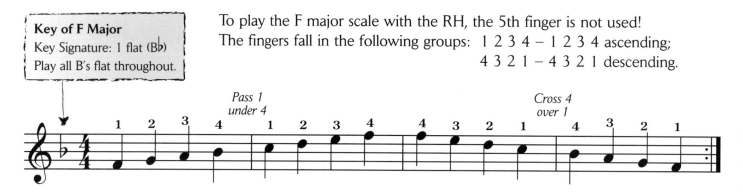

As soon as you play the thumb, move it under, carrying it at the base of the 3rd and 4th fingers until it is needed.

The fingering for the F major scale with the LH is the same as for all the scales you have studied so far: 5 4 3 2 1 – 3 2 1 ascending; 1 2 3 – 1 2 3 4 5 descending.

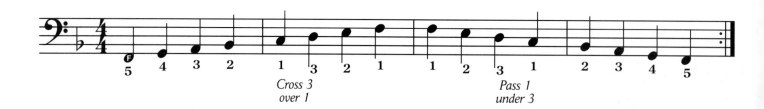

Technic Exercises: Preparation for Scale Playing

Key of F Major
Key Signature: 1 flat (B♭)
Play all B's flat throughout.

Play hands separately first.

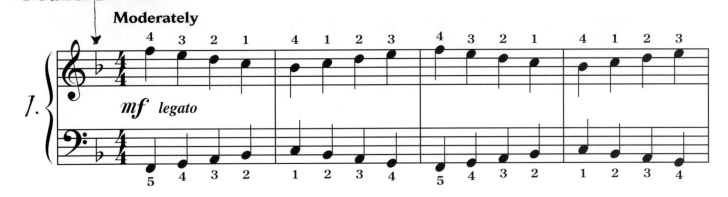

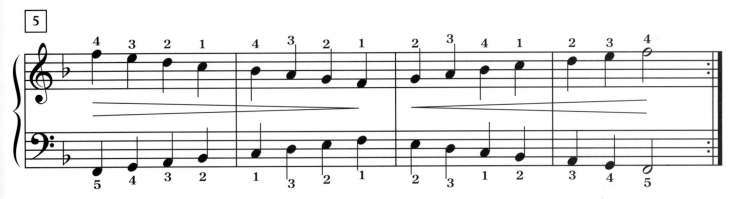

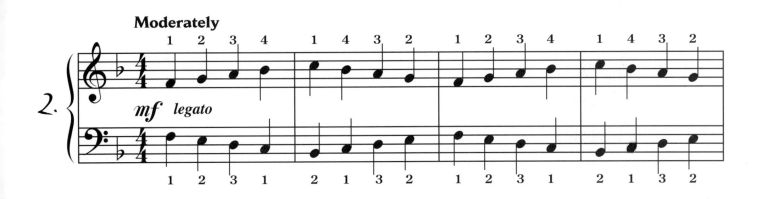

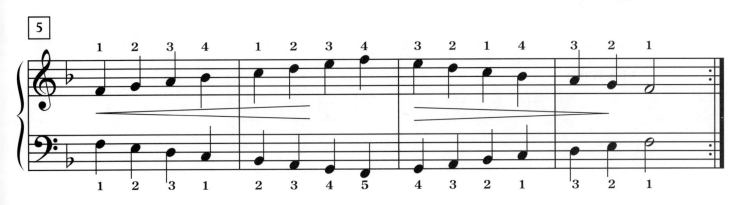

Write and Play Exercise

1. In the treble staff under the squares, write the notes of the F major scale.
Use whole notes. Add fingering above the notes and then play.

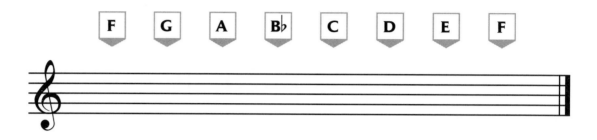

2. In the bass staff over the squares, write the notes of the F major scale.
Use whole notes. Add fingering below the notes and then play.

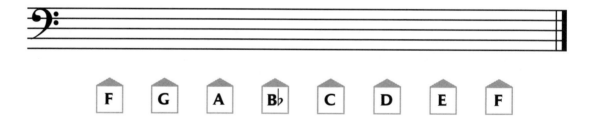

3. Write the name of each note in the square below it—then play and say the note names.

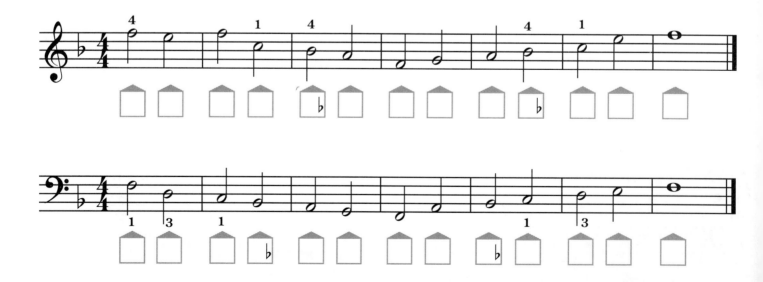

Practice Exercise: Sight Reading

1a.

b.

c.

d.

Moderately fast

2.

5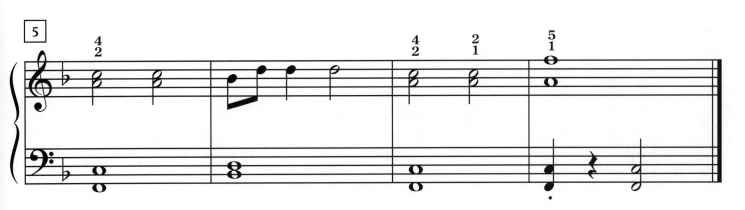

Accent Sign

> means *play with special emphasis!*

Little Brown Jug

Traditional

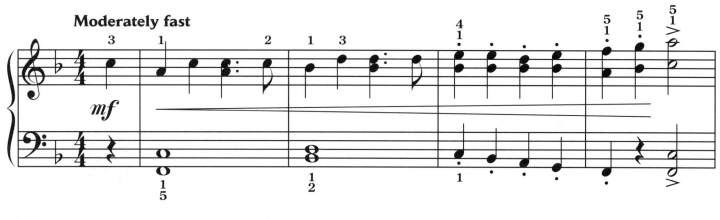

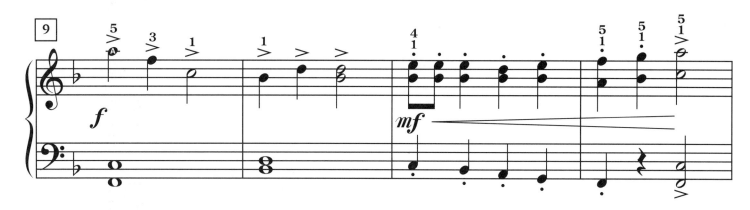

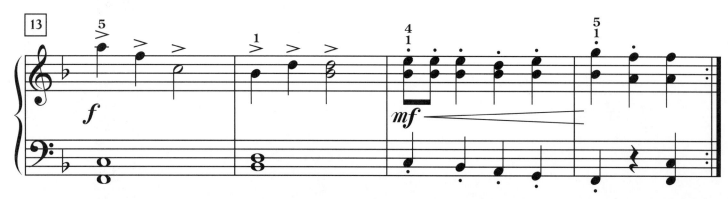

Casey Jones

Moderately

*Eighth notes may be played unevenly, in long-short pairs.

Primary Chords in F Major

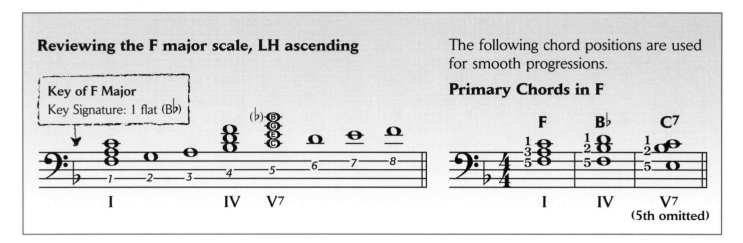

Play several times,
saying the chord names
and numerals aloud:

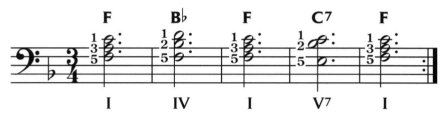

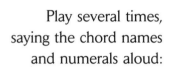

Chiapanecas
(Mexican Hand-Clapping Song)

Moderately fast

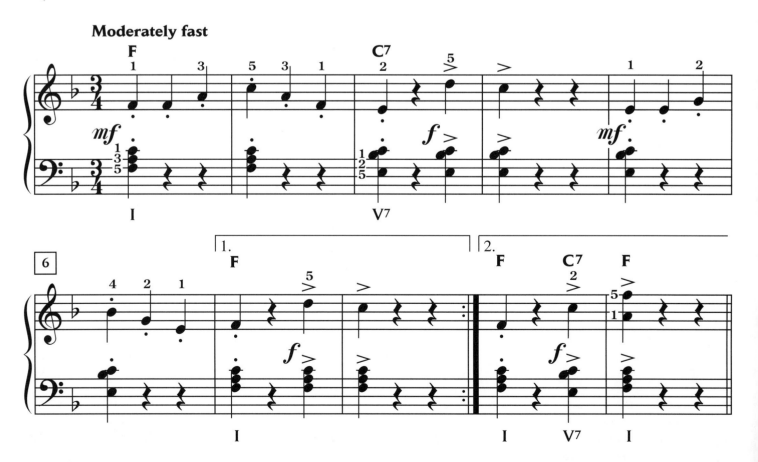

* The double dots inside the double bars indicate that everything between the double bars must be *repeated*. In this case, return to measure 11 and repeat.

Written Exercise: Away from the Keyboard

1. In the squares above the staff, write the names of the notes in each chord.

2. On the staff, circle the root of each chord.

3. On the line below the staff, write the name of the chord (**I, IV** or **V⁷**).

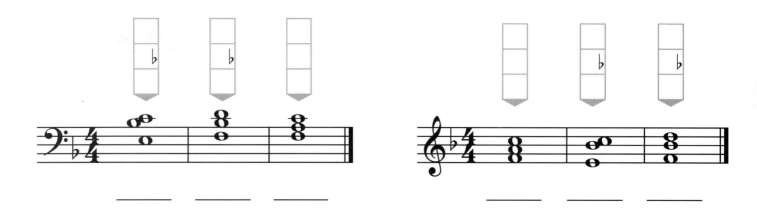

_____   _____   _____   _____   _____   _____

4. Draw a line from each box to its matching box in the adjacent column(s).

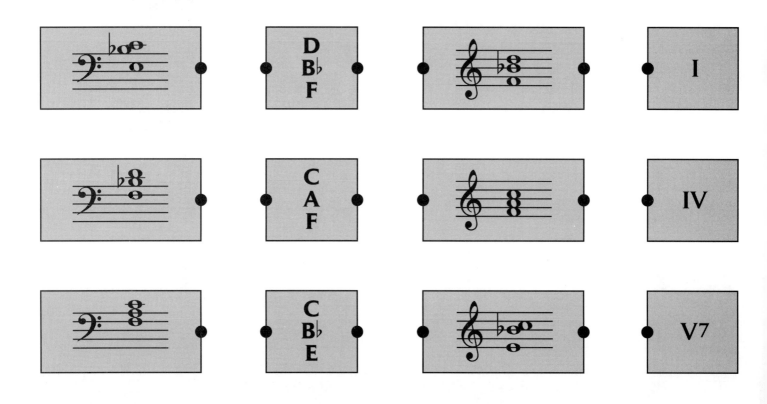

Auld Lang Syne

Old Scottish Air
Words by Robert Burns

Moderately slow

Practice Exercise: *Sight Reading*

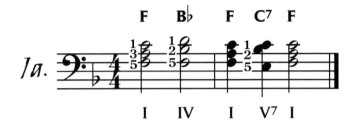

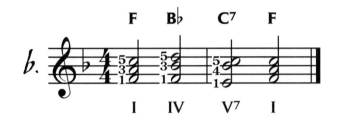

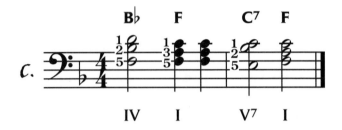

Moderately fast

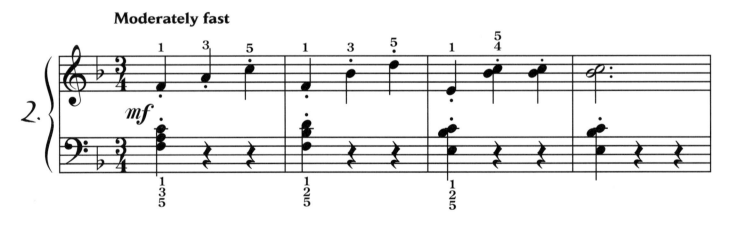

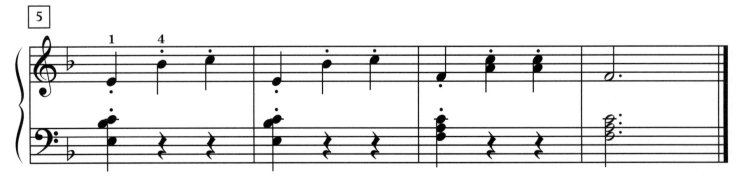

Clementine

Percy Montross

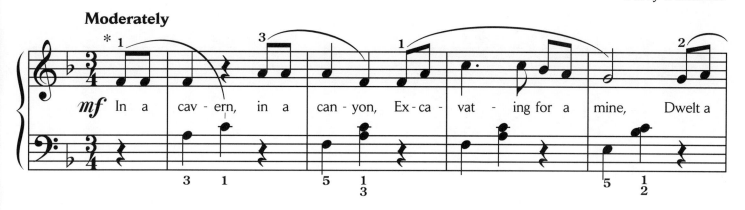

Moderately

mf In a cav - ern, in a can - yon, Ex - ca - vat - ing for a mine, Dwelt a

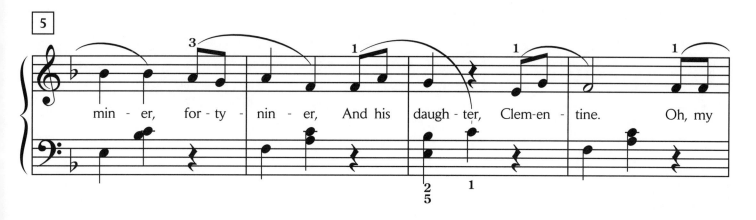

min - er, for - ty - nin - er, And his daugh - ter, Clem-en - tine. Oh, my

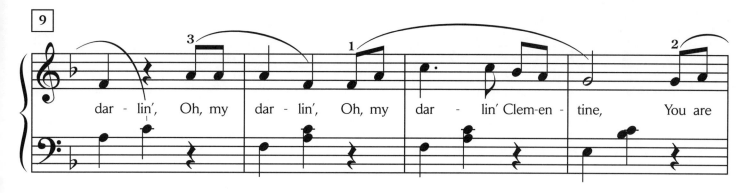

dar - lin', Oh, my dar - lin', Oh, my dar - lin' Clem-en - tine, You are

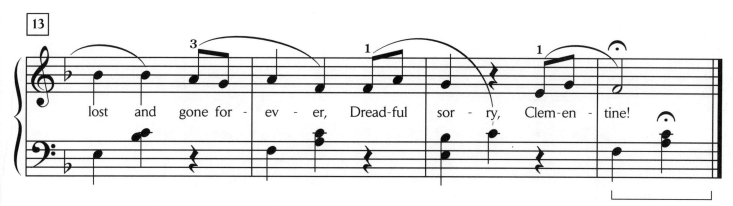

lost and gone for - ev - er, Dread-ful sor - ry, Clem-en - tine!

*Eighth notes may be played unevenly, in long-short pairs.

A New Style of Bass

Play this several times before beginning *O Sole Mio:*

Moderately slow

COUNT: 1 & 2 & 3 & 4 &   1 & 2 & 3 & 4 &   1 & 2 & 3 & 4 &   1 & 2 & 3 & 4 &

O Sole Mio!

From Enrico Caruso to a recording entitled "In Concert," by José Carreras, Plácido Domingo and Luciano Pavarotti, this great old favorite has provided tenors with surefire encore material. "There's No Tomorrow," popular in the 50s and 60s, was sung to this melody.

Eduardo di Capua

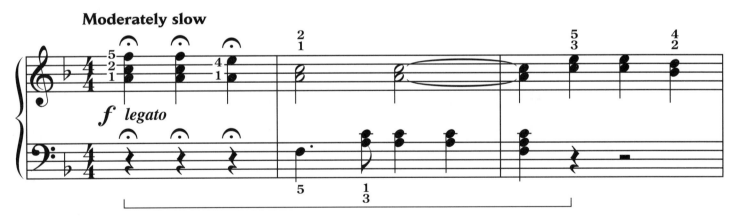

Moderately slow

f *legato*

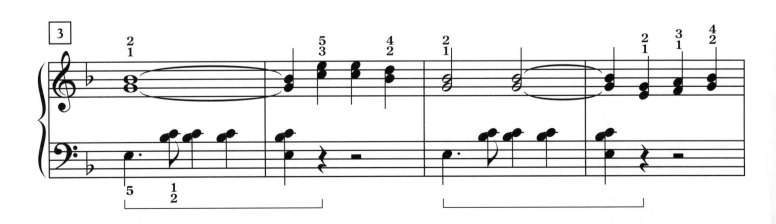

*Arpeggiated Chords

When a wavy line appears before a chord, the chord is **arpeggiated** (broken or rolled). Play the lowest note first, and quickly add the next higher notes one at a time until the chord is complete. The first note is played on the beat.

Eighth Rest

𝄾 Rest for the value of an eighth note.

Alexander's Ragtime Band

Irving Berlin was one of America's most successful songwriters of the 20th century, even though he couldn't read music and played piano using only the black keys. "Alexander's Ragtime Band" is one of his most popular pieces and contains quotes from Stephen Foster's "Old Folks at Home."

Irving Berlin
(1888–1989)

Come on and hear, come on and hear Al - ex - an - der's Rag - time

Band. Come on and hear, come on and hear, It's the best band in the

land. They can play a bu-gle call like you nev-er heard be-fore, So nat-u-ral that you

want to go to war. That's just the best-est band what am,

*Eighth notes may be played unevenly, in long-short pairs.

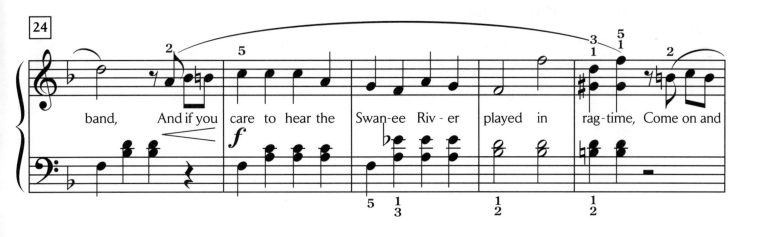

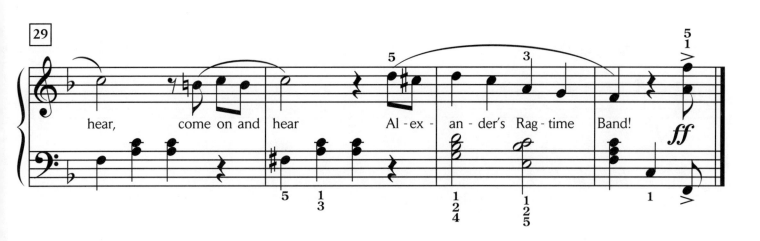

Unit 6

The Key of A Minor

The Key of A Minor (Relative of C Major)

Every major key has a **relative minor** key that has the same *key signature.*

The relative minor begins on the *6th* tone of the major scale. Therefore, the relative minor of C major is A minor.

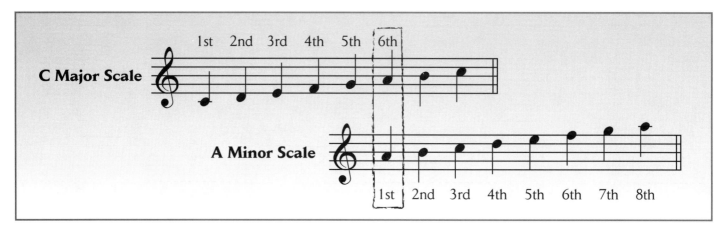

Because the keys of C major and A minor have the same key signature (no sharps or flats), they are relatives.

The minor scale shown above is called the **natural minor** scale. It uses only notes that are found in the **relative major** scale.

The A Harmonic Minor Scale

The most frequently used minor scale is the **harmonic minor.** In this scale, the 7th tone is raised ascending and descending.

The raised 7th in the key of A minor is G♯. It is not included in the key signature, but is written as an **accidental*** each time it occurs.

Key of A Minor
Key Signature: no ♯, no ♭

Practice the A harmonic minor scale hands separately. Begin slowly and gradually increase speed.

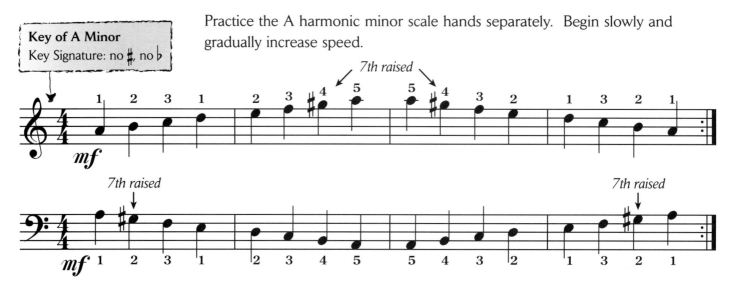

Important! After you have learned the A harmonic minor scale hands separately, you may play the hands together in contrary motion, by combining the two staffs above.

*An *accidental* is a sharp or flat that is not in the key signature. A natural sign is also an accidental.

Write and Play Exercise

1. In the treble staff under the squares, write the notes of the A harmonic minor scale. Use whole notes. Add fingering above the notes and then play.

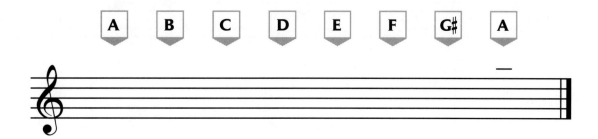

2. In the bass staff over the squares, write the notes of the A harmonic minor scale. Use whole notes. Add fingering below the notes and then play.

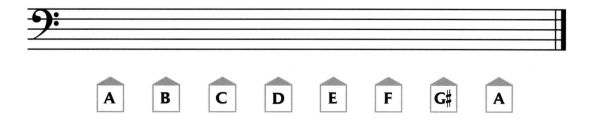

3. Write the name of each note in the square below it—then play and say the note names.

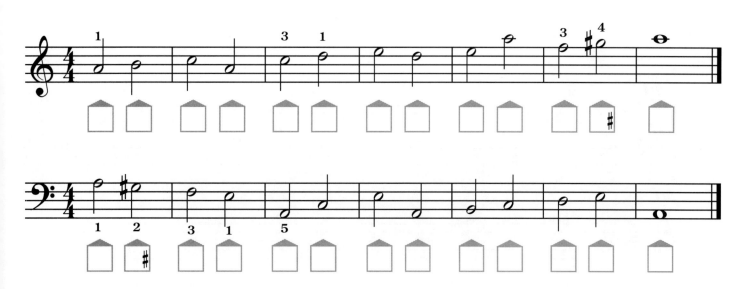

Practice Exercise: Sight Reading

Jericho

More Syncopated Notes

Spiritual

Key of A Minor*
Key Signature: no ♯, no ♭

Moderately fast

mf

f

* To determine whether a piece is in a major key or its relative minor, look at the end of the piece.
  It will end on the key note or chord. This piece has no sharps or flats in the key signature and
  it ends on A (an A minor chord); therefore, the piece is in the key of A minor.

Major and Minor Triads

Major triads and minor triads each consist of a root, 3rd and 5th.

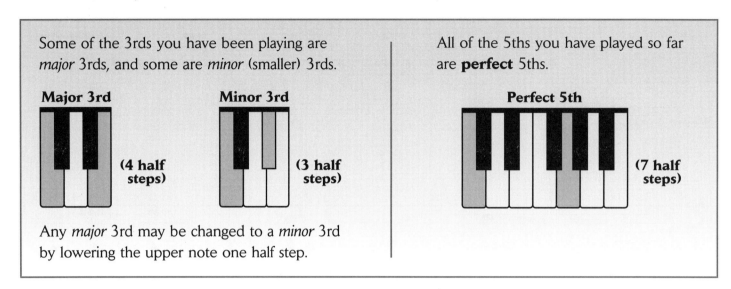

Some of the 3rds you have been playing are *major* 3rds, and some are *minor* (smaller) 3rds.

Major 3rd (4 half steps)   **Minor 3rd** (3 half steps)

Any *major* 3rd may be changed to a *minor* 3rd by lowering the upper note one half step.

All of the 5ths you have played so far are **perfect** 5ths.

Perfect 5th (7 half steps)

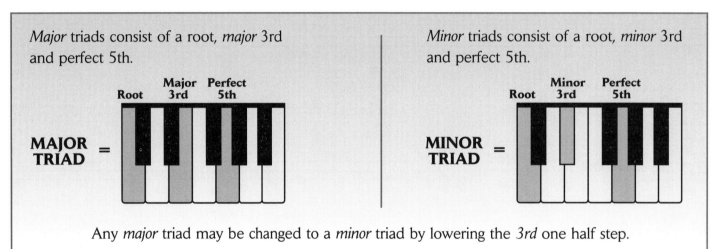

Major triads consist of a root, *major* 3rd and perfect 5th.

MAJOR TRIAD = Root / Major 3rd / Perfect 5th

Minor triads consist of a root, *minor* 3rd and perfect 5th.

MINOR TRIAD = Root / Minor 3rd / Perfect 5th

Any *major* triad may be changed to a *minor* triad by lowering the *3rd* one half step.

1. Play the following triads with RH 1 3 5. Say "C major triad, C minor triad," as you play each pair.

2. Play the following triads with LH 5 3 1. Say "C major triad, C minor triad," as you play each pair.

Modern Sounds

This piece uses the key of C major and its relative minor key (A minor).

It begins with the RH and LH moving up and down the keyboard in major and minor thirds. All the thirds are fingered with the 2nd and 4th fingers. RH and LH 2s are on neighboring white keys.

In the second section, only the RH plays thirds. The LH plays fifths with 5 and 1.

Key of C Major
Key Signature: no ♯, no ♭

Key of A Minor
Key Signature: no ♯, no ♭

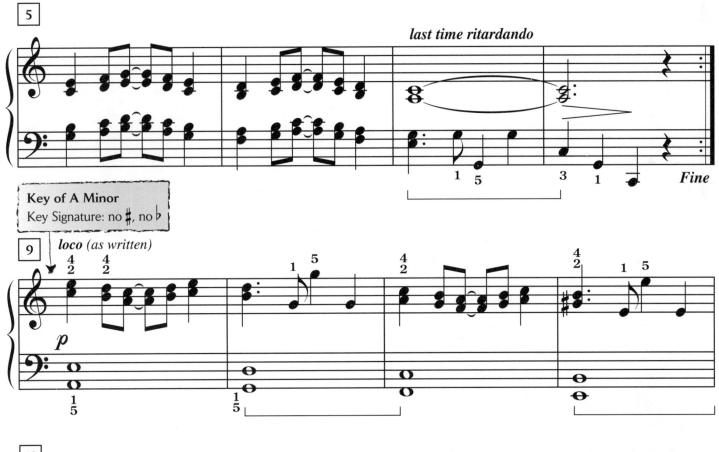

D. C. al Fine

Key of C Major
Key Signature: no #, no ♭

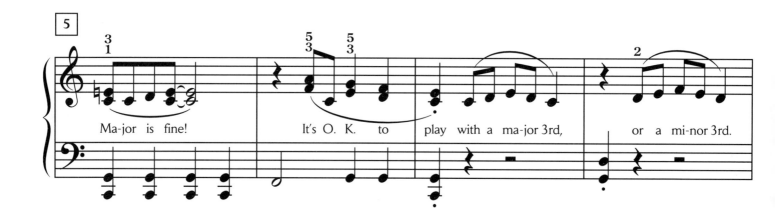

*Eighth notes may be played unevenly, in long-short pairs.

Introducing Overlapping Pedal

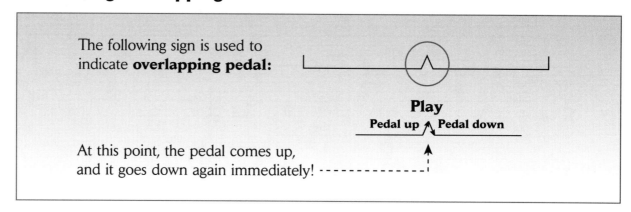

The following sign is used to indicate **overlapping pedal:**

Play
Pedal up ⋀ Pedal down

At this point, the pedal comes up, and it goes down again immediately! - - - - - - - - - - - -

Practice the following exercises before playing *Greensleeves.*

Greensleeves

Moderately slow

mp

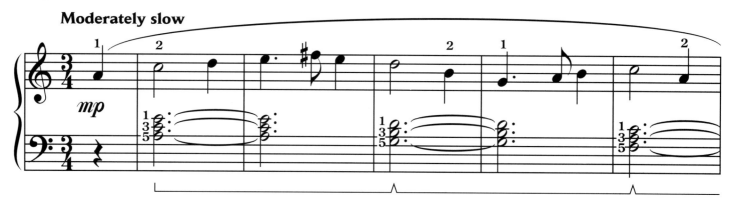

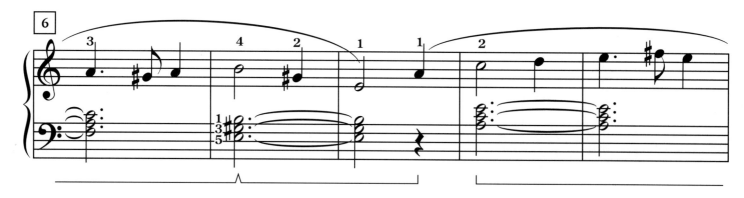

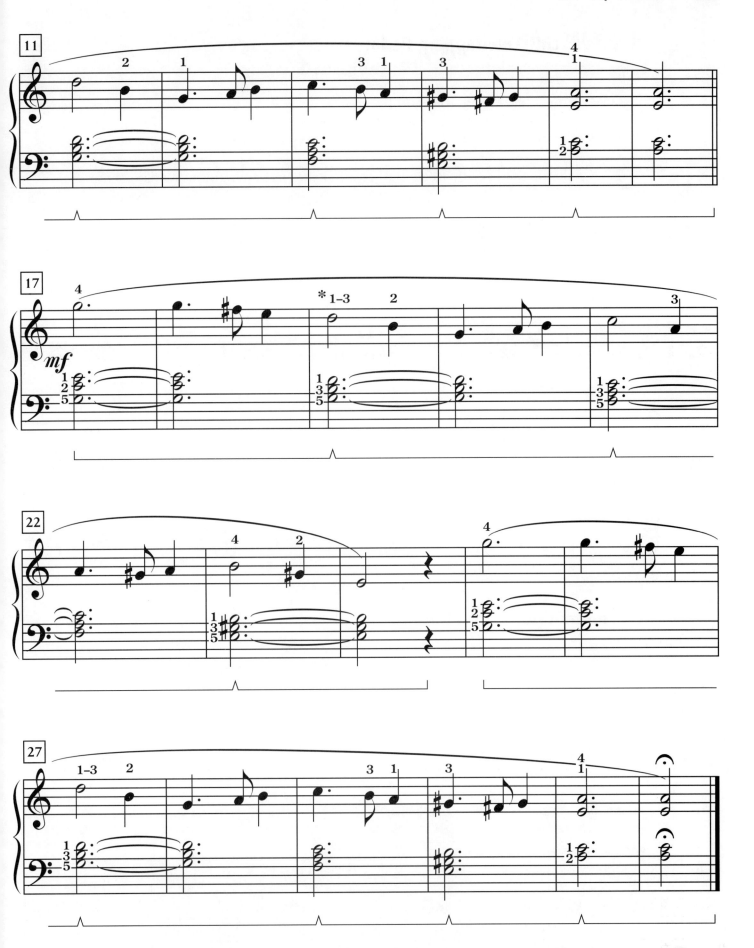

*Finger substitution: While holding the note down with finger 1, change to finger 3 on the 2nd beat.

Written Exercise: Away from the Keyboard

Review Major and Minor Triads on page 76.

1. Circle the triad on the bass staff that matches its name in the middle column.

2. Circle the triad on the treble staff that matches its name in the middle column.

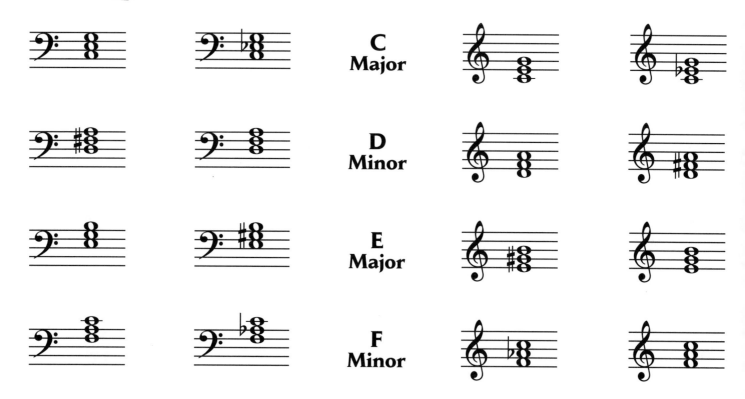

Primary Chords in A Minor

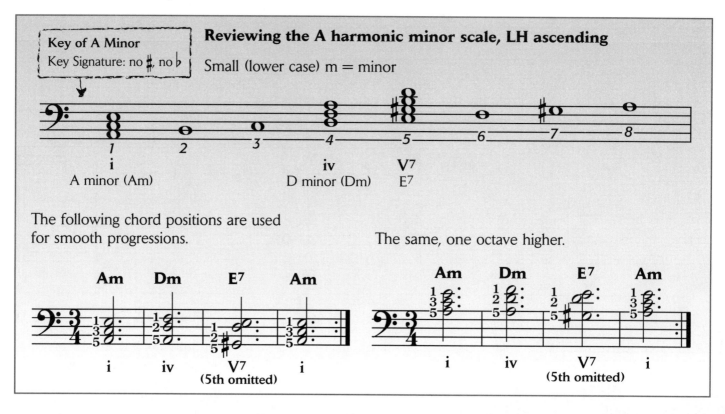

Go Down, Moses

Spiritual

Key of A Minor
Key Signature: no ♯, no ♭

More Syncopated Notes

*N.C. = no chord

Practice Exercise: **Sight Reading**

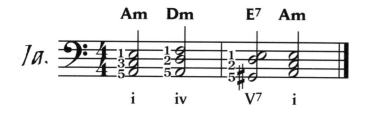

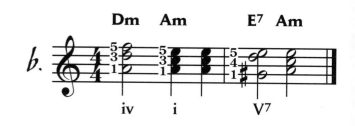

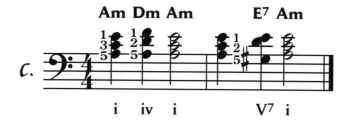

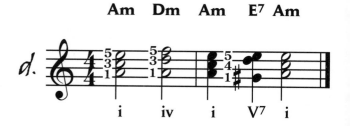

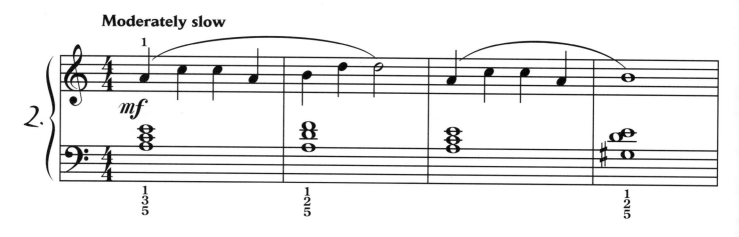

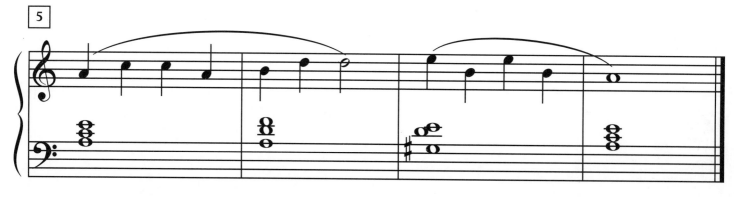

Written Exercise: Away from the Keyboard

1. In the squares above the staff, write the names of the notes in each chord.

2. On the staff, circle the root of each chord.

3. On the line below the staff, write the name of the chord (**i, iv** or **V⁷**).

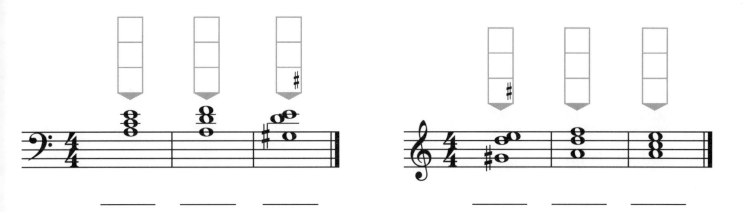

_____   _____   _____   _____   _____   _____

4. Draw a line from each box to its matching box in the adjacent column(s).

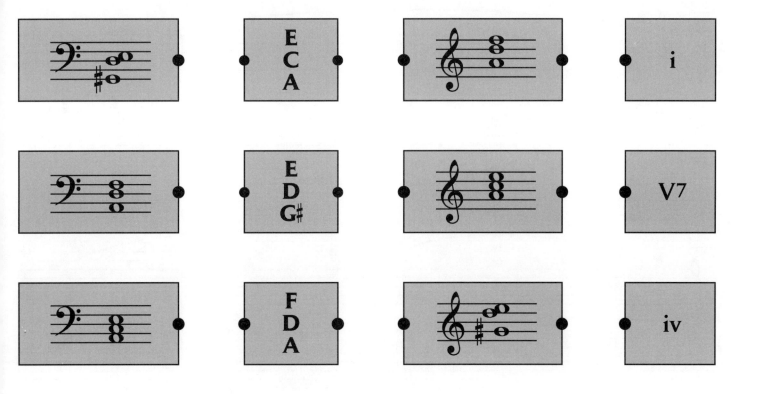

LH Review: Block Chords and Broken Chords in A Minor

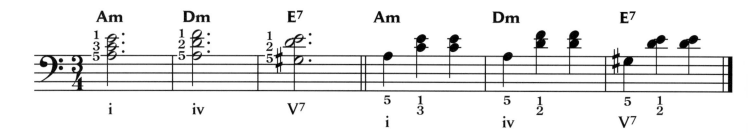

Tumbalalaika

Traditional

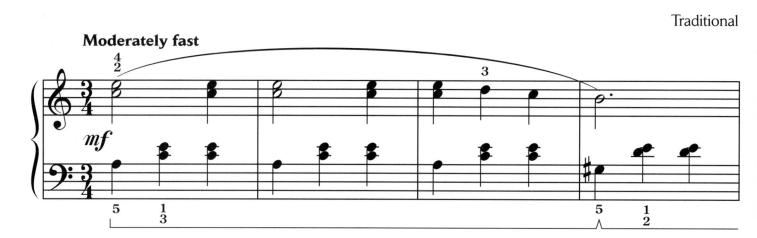

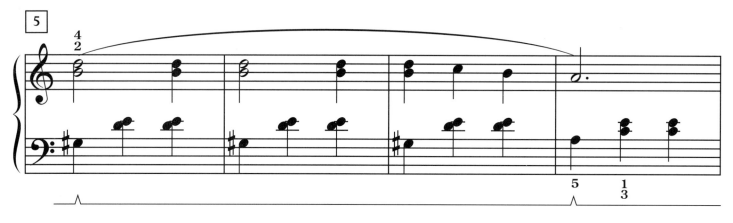

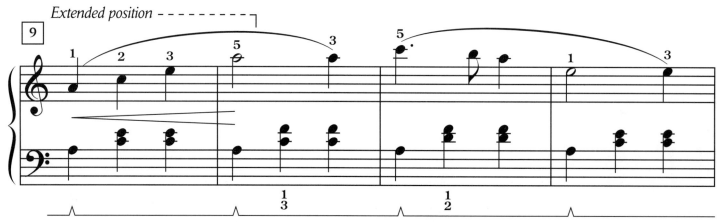

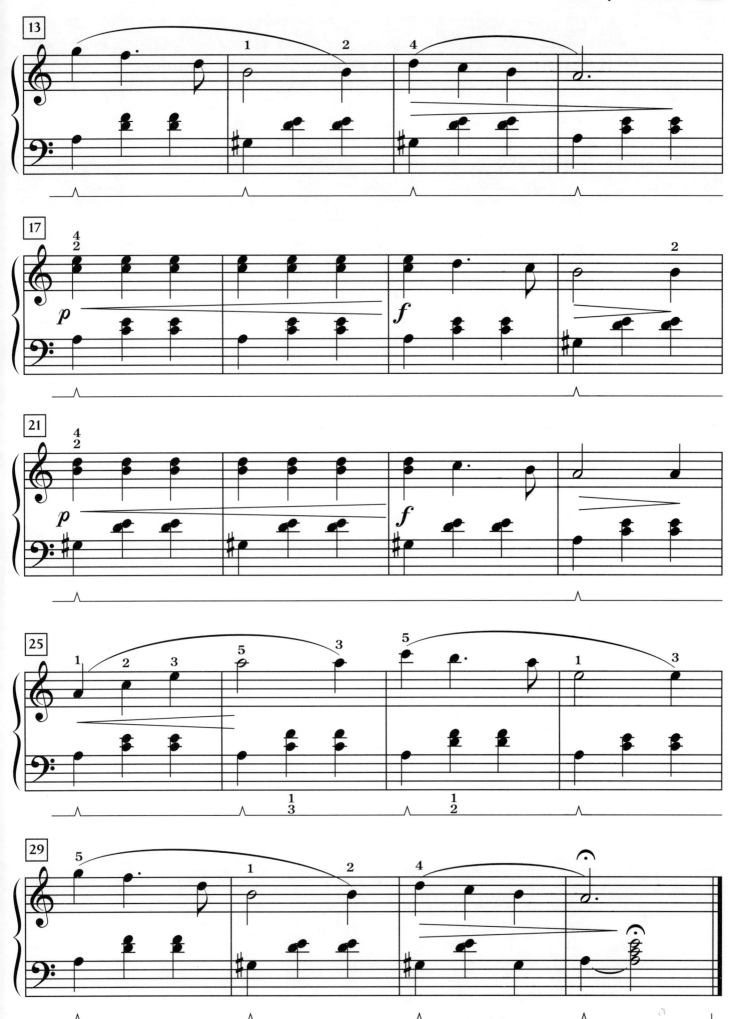

Unit 7

The Key of D Minor

D minor is the relative minor of F major. Both keys have the same key signature (1 flat, B♭).

Remember: The relative minor begins on the *6th* tone of the major scale.

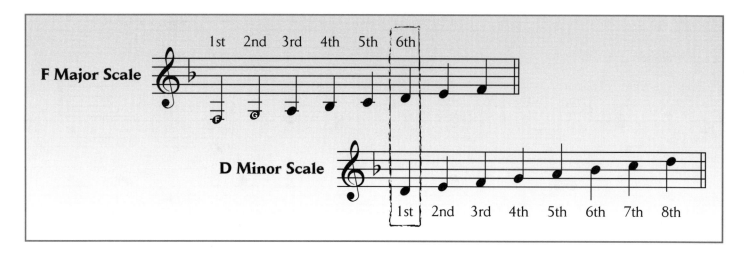

The minor scale shown above is the *natural minor* scale. Remember, the natural minor uses only notes that are found in the *relative major* scale.

The D Harmonic Minor Scale

In the *harmonic minor* scale, the 7th tone is raised ascending and descending.

The raised 7th in the key of D minor is C♯. It is not included in the key signature, but is written as an accidental each time it occurs.

Practice the D harmonic minor scale hands separately. Begin slowly and gradually increase speed.

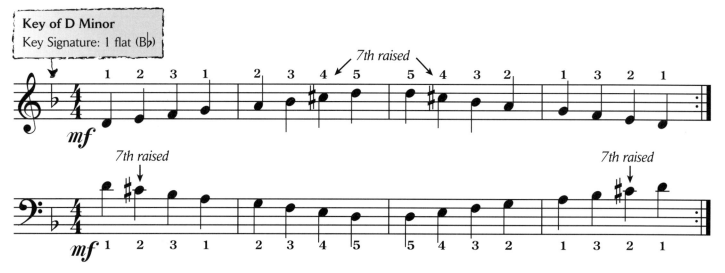

Important! After you have learned the D harmonic minor scale hands separately, you may play the hands together in contrary motion, by combining the two staffs above.

Write and Play Exercise

1. In the treble staff under the squares, write the notes of the D harmonic minor scale. Use whole notes. Add fingering above the notes and then play.

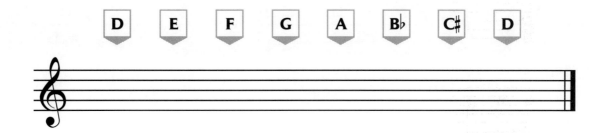

2. In the bass staff over the squares, write the notes of the D harmonic minor scale. Use whole notes. Add fingering below the notes and then play.

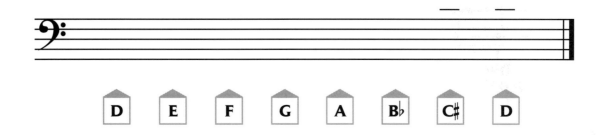

3. Write the name of each note in the square below it—then play and say the note names.

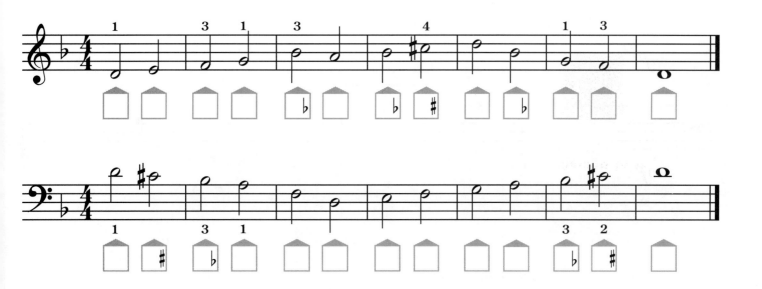

Practice Exercise: Sight Reading

1a.
b.

c.
d.

2.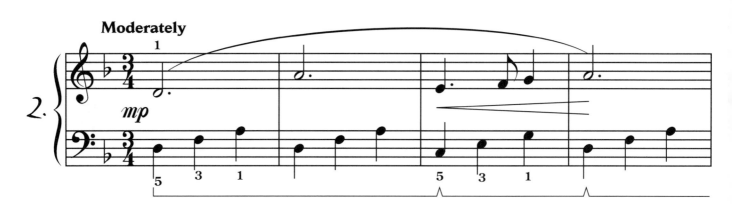

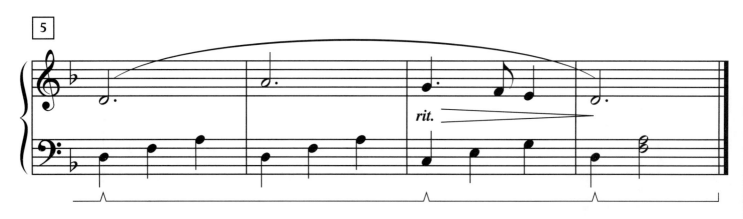

Scarborough Fair

Key of D Minor
Key Signature: 1 flat (B♭)

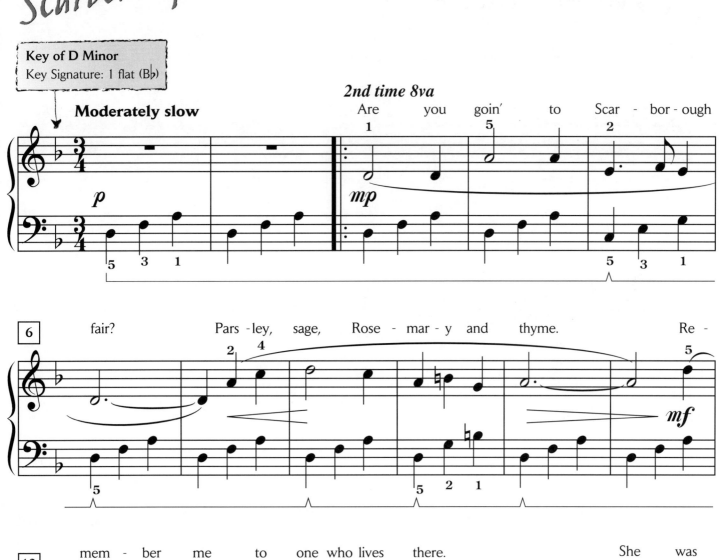

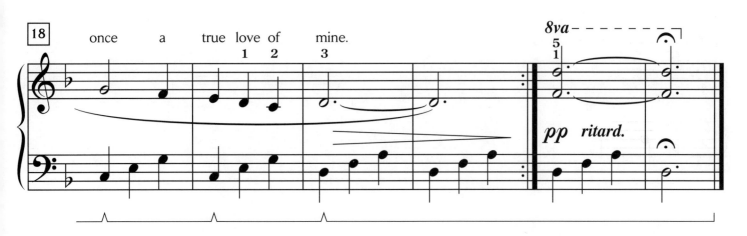

Primary Chords in D Minor

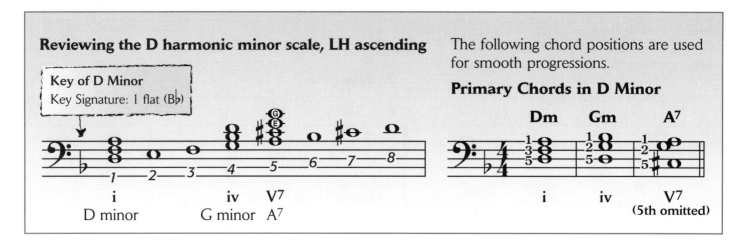

Reviewing the D harmonic minor scale, LH ascending

Key of D Minor
Key Signature: 1 flat (B♭)

i   iv   V7
D minor   G minor   A7

The following chord positions are used for smooth progressions.

Primary Chords in D Minor

Dm   Gm   A7

i   iv   V7
(5th omitted)

Play several times,
saying the chord names
and numerals aloud:

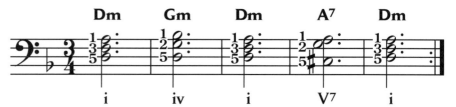

i   iv   i   V7   i

D Minor Progression with broken i, iv and V7 chords

Play several times.

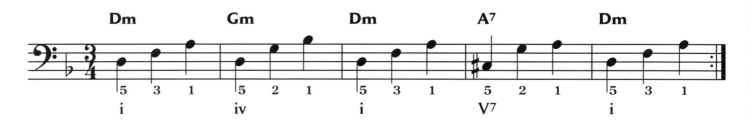

i   iv   i   V7   i

Raisins and Almonds

Folk Song

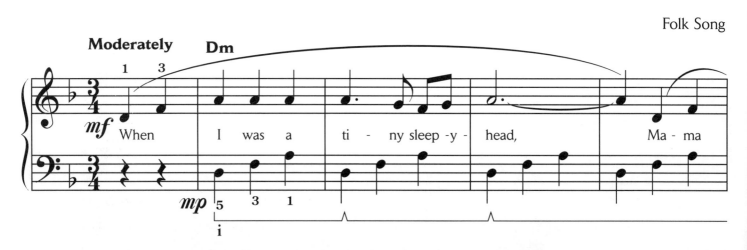

Moderately

mf When   I   was   a   ti - ny sleep -y- head,   Ma - ma

mp

i

Practice Exercise: Sight Reading

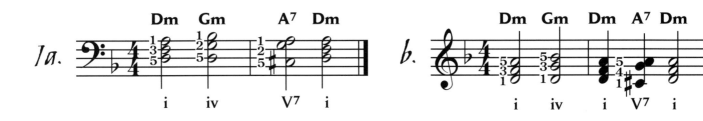

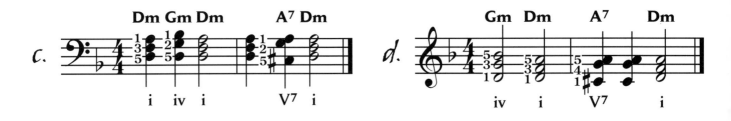

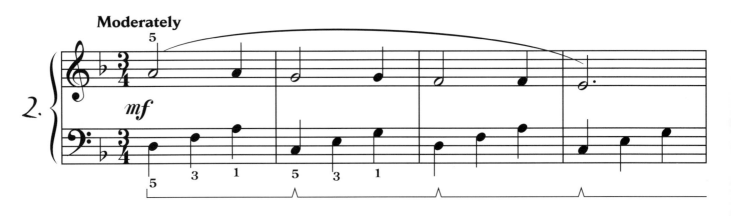

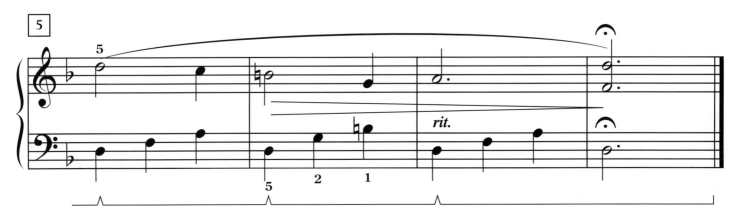

Written Exercise: Away from the Keyboard

1. In the squares above the staff, write the names of the notes in each chord.

2. On the staff, circle the root of each chord.

3. On the line below the staff, write the name of the chord (**i, iv** or **V⁷**).

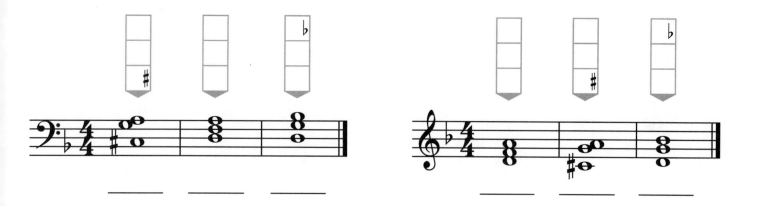

4. Draw a line from each box to its matching box in the adjacent column(s).

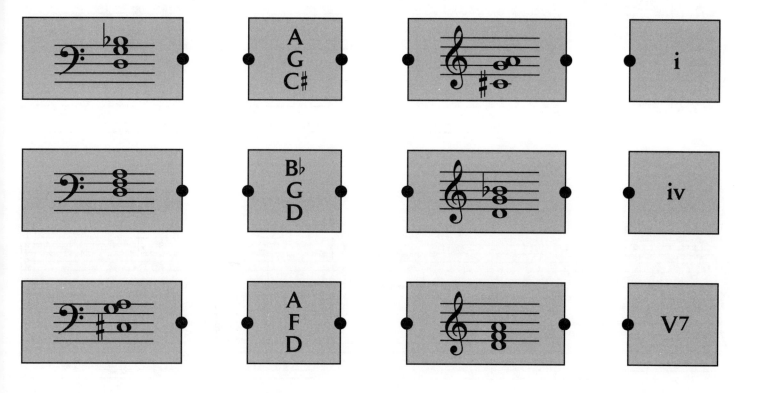

New Time Signature

C means **common time,**
which is the same as $\frac{4}{4}$ time.

Introduction and Dance

This very popular folk tune uses mostly the primary chords in D minor, but you will also find two D major triads, plus the V^7 and I chords in A major and F major.

The popular song "Those Were the Days" was based on this old folk melody.

Folk Song

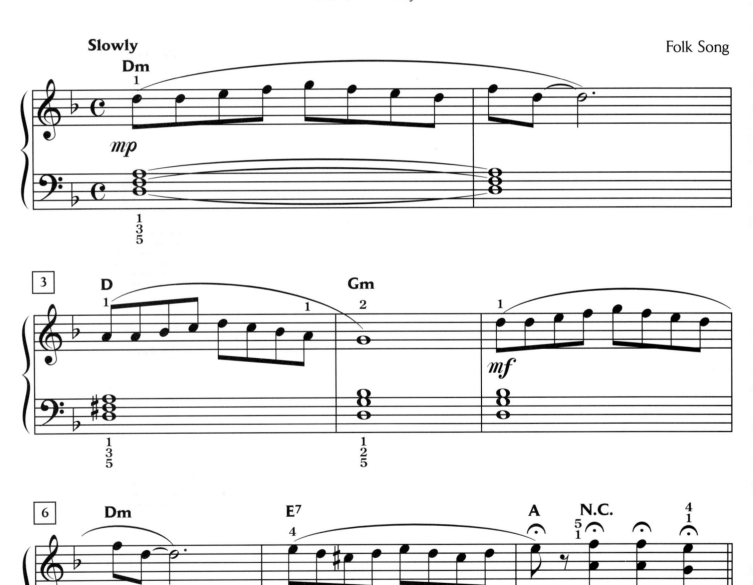

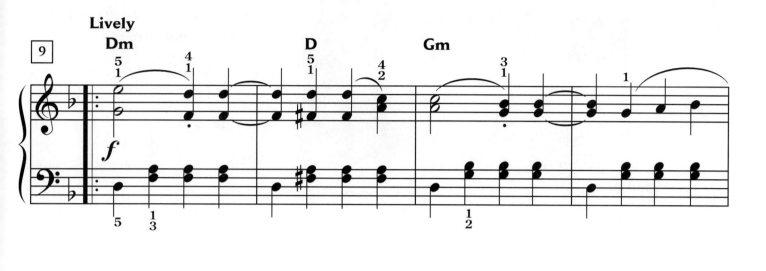

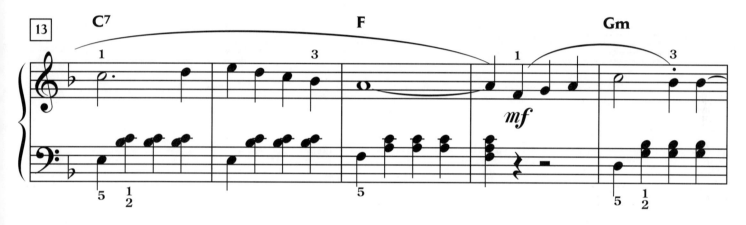

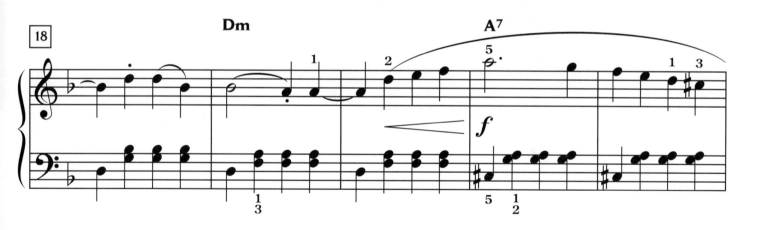

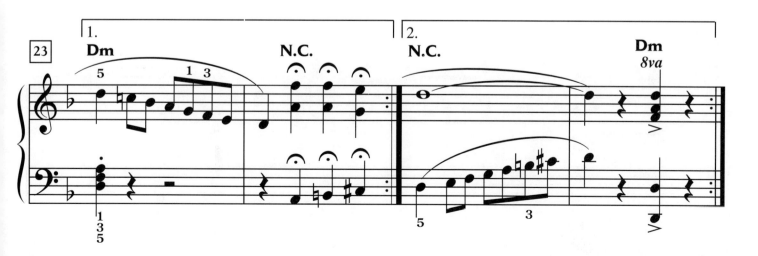

Hungarian Dance No. 5

Brahms originally composed the Hungarian Dances for piano duet. These dances capture the spirit, style and rhythmic flair of Hungarian gypsy music. He had probably heard many of the melodies performed in an improvisational setting by gypsy bands.

Johannes Brahms
(1833–1897)

Moderately fast

Unit 8

Reviewing Notes, Chords and Technical Patterns

Written Exercise: Away from the Keyboard

Solve the crossword puzzle by writing the names of the notes in the squares.

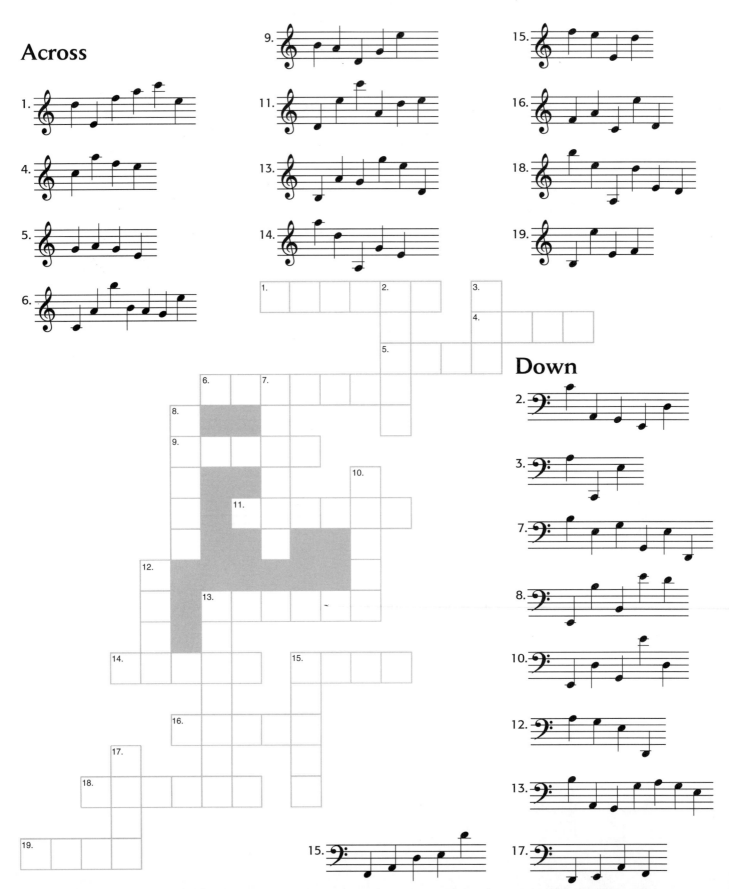

Practice Exercise: Sight Reading

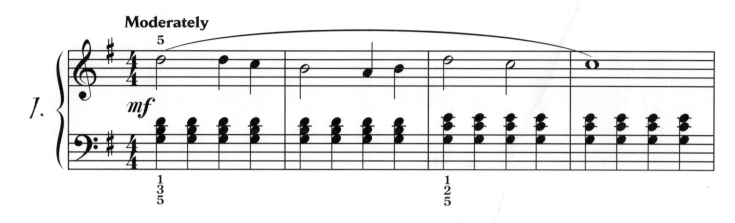

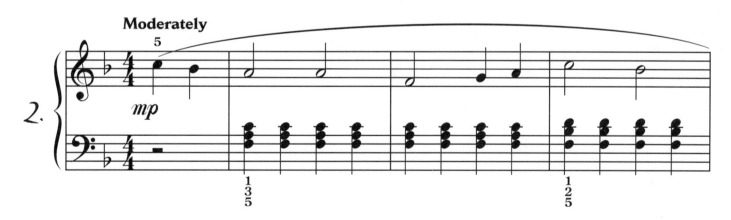

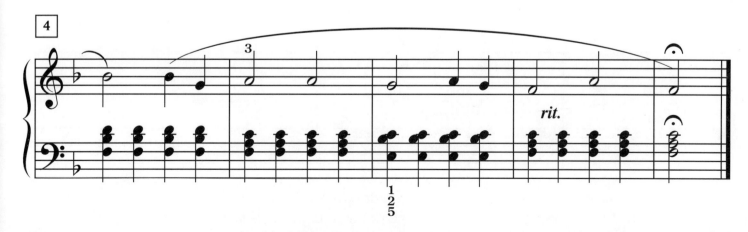

He's Got the Whole World in His Hands

More Syncopated Notes

Count: 1 & 2 & 3 & 4 &

Key of G Major
Key Signature: 1 sharp (F♯)

Moderately & rhythmically

Spiritual

Key of C Major
Key Signature: no ♯, no ♭

This piece reviews the I, IV and V⁷ chords of the keys of G major, C major and F major.
It also reviews syncopated notes, in preparation for *The Entertainer,* on pages 104–105.

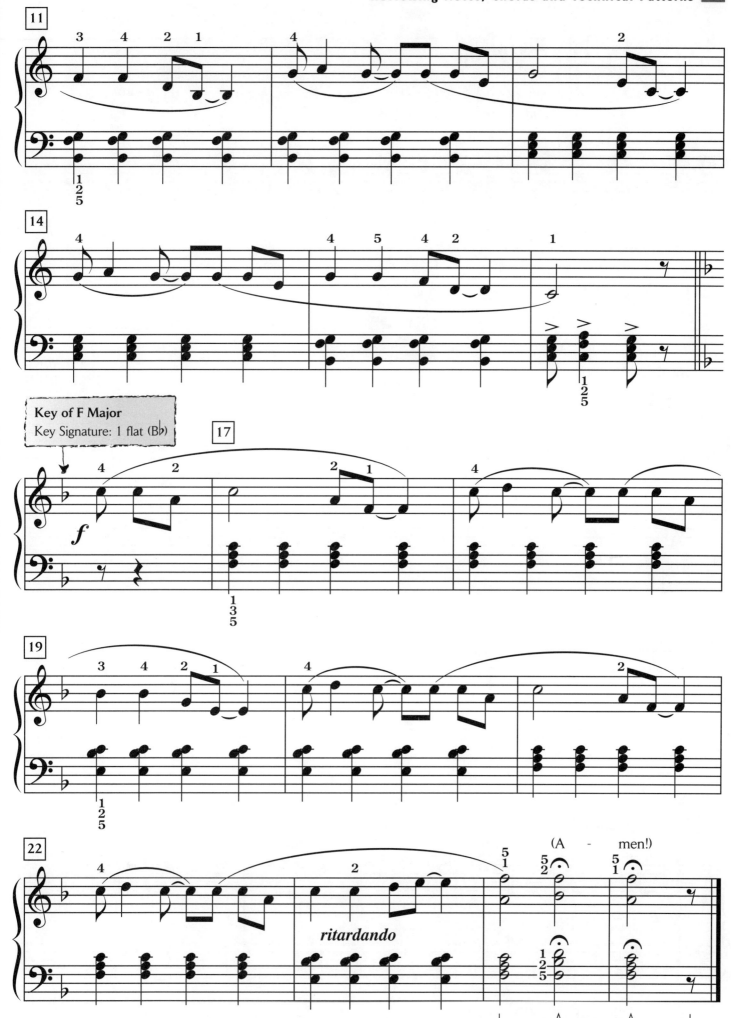

Key of F Major
Key Signature: 1 flat (B♭)

Technic Exercise: *Warm-Up*

Practice many times, very slowly. These four measures contain everything new that you will find in the LH of *The Entertainer!*

The Entertainer

With the release of the movie, "The Sting," in 1973, Scott Joplin took his place as one of America's greatest composers of ragtime. His ragtime contains elements of both classical and popular styles and continues to be enjoyed throughout the world today.

Scott Joplin
(1868–1917)

Not fast!*

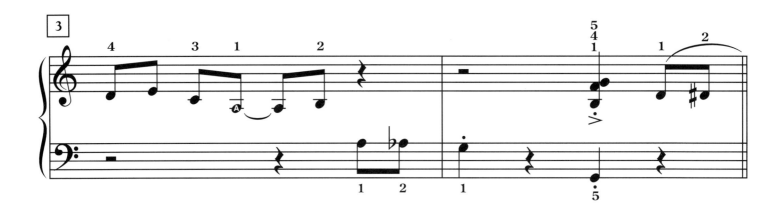

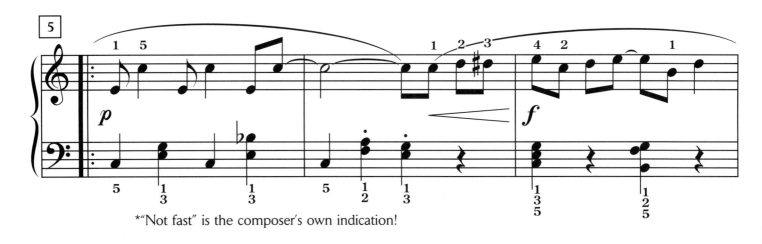

*"Not fast" is the composer's own indication!

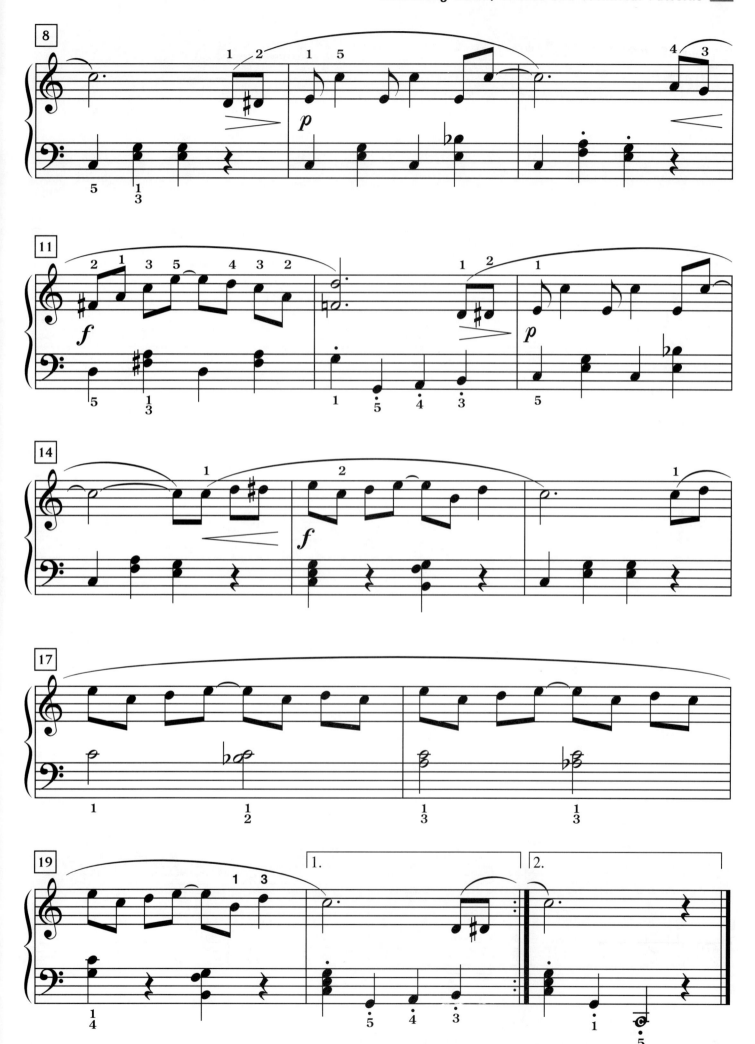

Theme from Solace
(A Mexican Serenade)

Scott Joplin
(1868–1917)

More Syncopated Notes

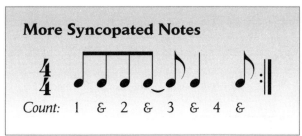

Count: 1 & 2 & 3 & 4 &

Very slow march time

mf

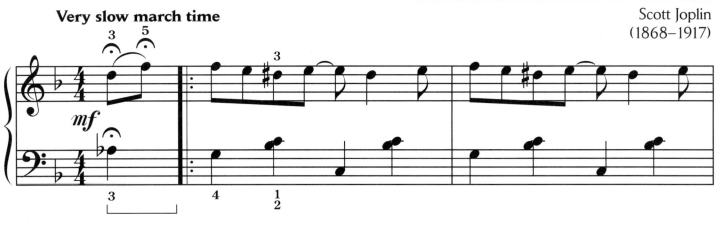

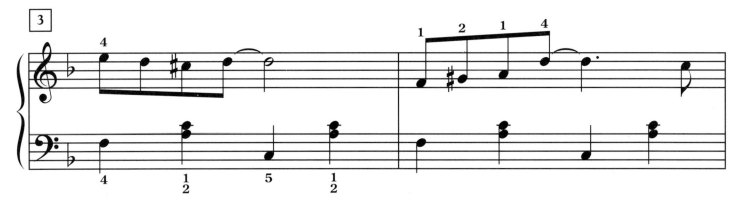

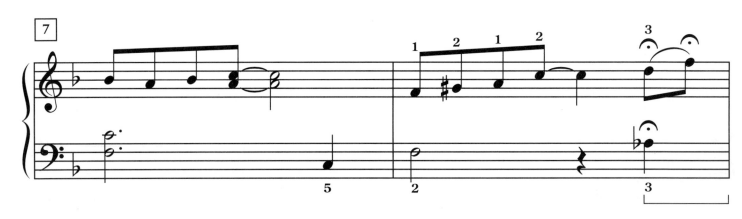

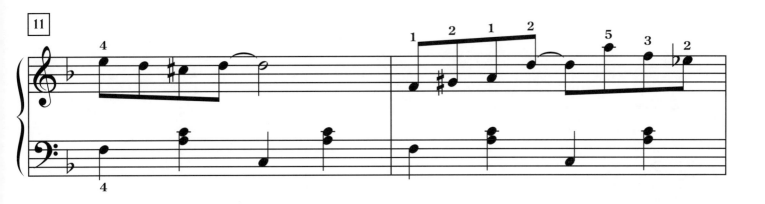

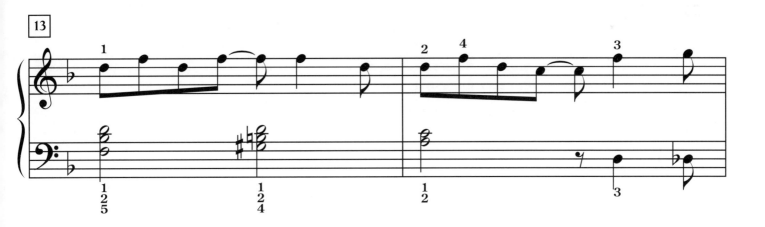

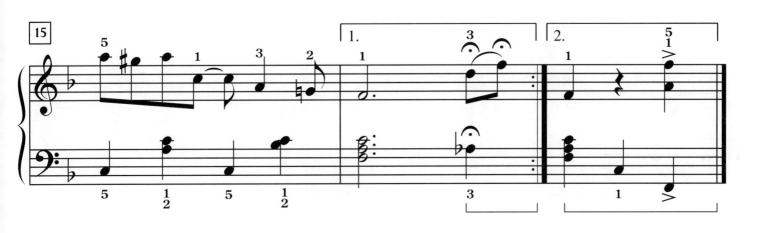

Technic Exercise: Passing 1 Under 2

It is important to develop the ability to pass 1 under 2 and 1 under 3 with a relaxed wrist, and with no twisting motion of the hand. Play the exercises slowly at first, then faster.

1. Write the finger numbers *over* each of the following notes, so that 1 will pass under 2, as shown in the first example.

2. Write the names of the notes in the boxes, then play with the RH.

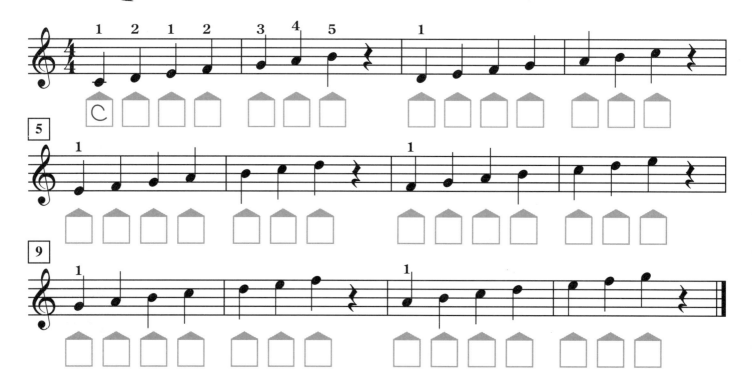

3. Write the finger numbers *under* each of the following notes, so that 1 will pass under 2, as shown in the first example.

4. Write the names of the notes in the boxes, then play with the LH.

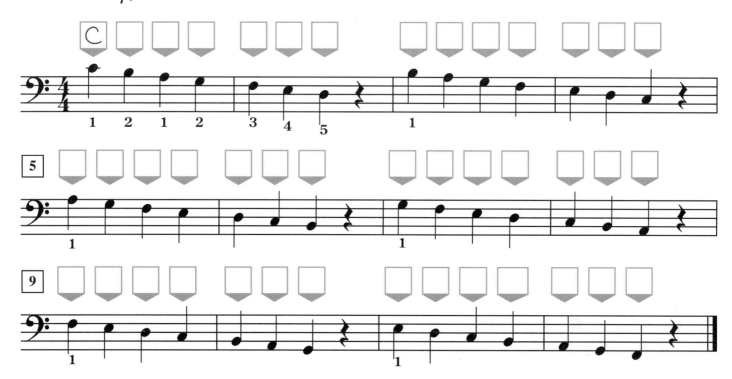

Technic Exercise: Passing 1 Under 3

1. Write the finger numbers *over* each of the following notes, so that 1 will pass under 3, as shown in the first example.

2. Write the names of the notes in the boxes, then play with the RH.

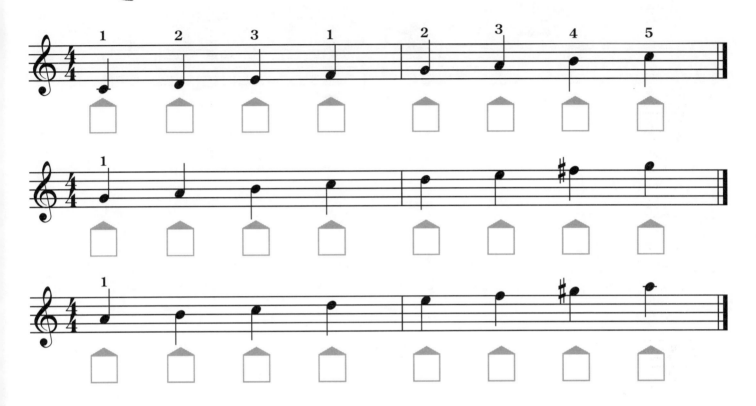

3. Write the finger numbers *under* each of the following notes, so that 1 will pass under 3, as shown in the first example.

4. Write the names of the notes in the boxes, then play with the LH.

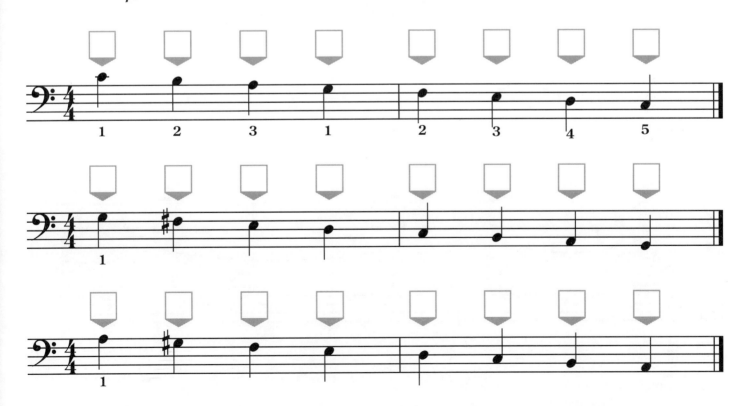

Light and Blue

Moderate blues tempo

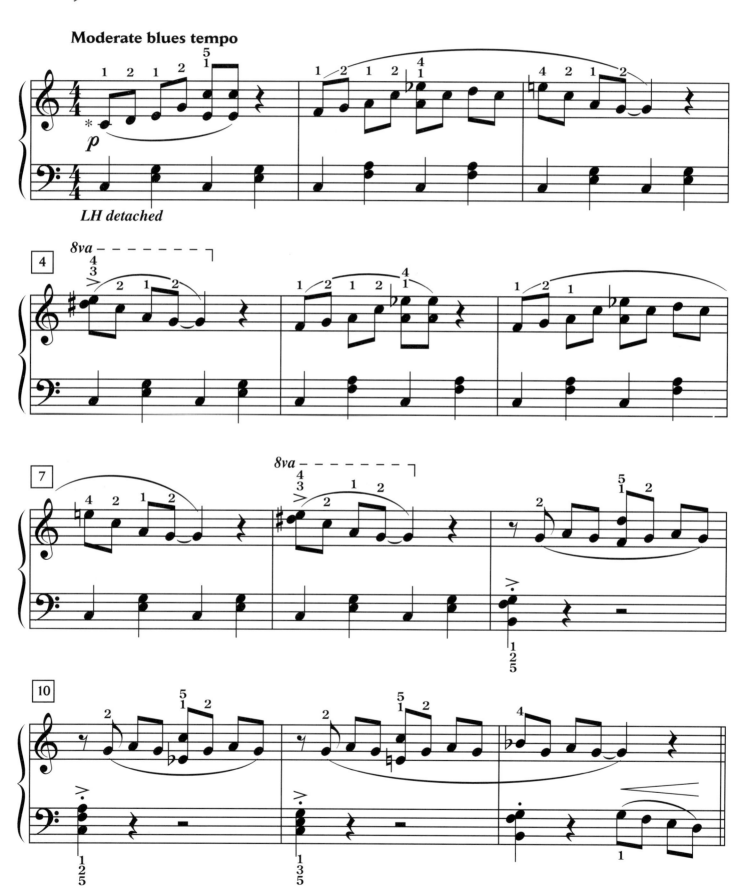

LH detached

*Eighth notes may be played unevenly, in long-short pairs.

*Optional: The repeat may be played *8va,* with notes marked *8va* played *as written.*

Hungarian Rhapsody No. 2 (Theme)

Liszt was recognized as the greatest pianist of his day. His concerts were always filled with drama and showmanship. He composed over 1000 works for piano; the Hungarian Rhapsody No. 2 is one of his most famous.

Franz Liszt
(1811–1886)

Not too fast, with rhythmic emphasis

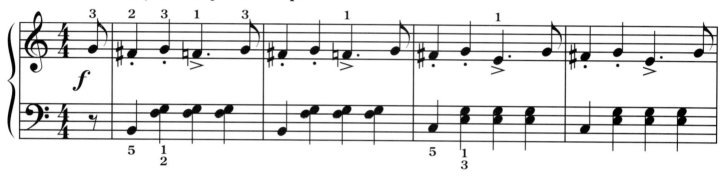

5

9 **A little faster**

13 *poco rit.*

gradually faster and faster to the end

Unit 9

New Rhythms and Time Signatures

The Chromatic Scale

The **chromatic scale** is made up entirely of *half steps*. It goes up and down, using every key, black and white. It may begin on any note.

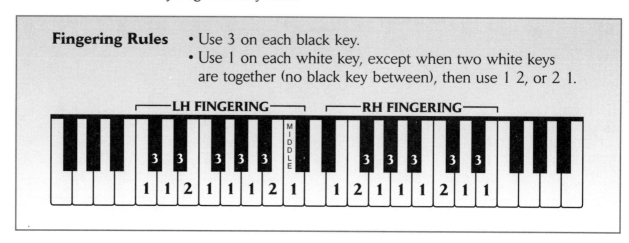

1. Looking at the keyboard above, play the chromatic scale with the LH. Begin on middle C and go *down* one octave.

2. Looking at the keyboard above, play the chromatic scale with the RH. Begin on E above middle C and go *up* one octave.

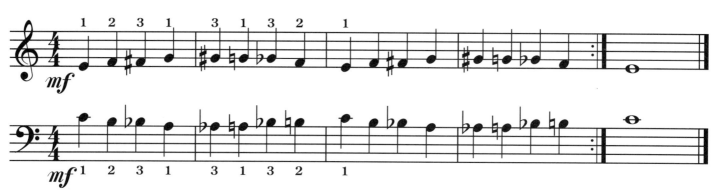

One-Octave Chromatic Scale
Play several times daily!

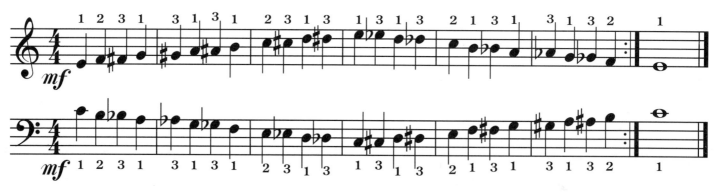

It is easy and fun to play the chromatic scale in *contrary motion*! When the RH begins on E and the LH on C, as above, both hands play the same numbered fingers simultaneously.

Village Dance

Folk Tune

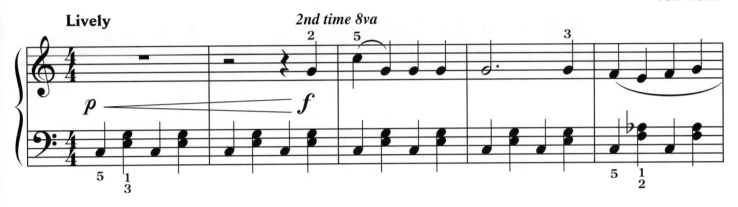

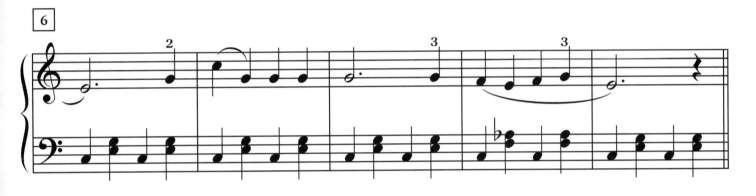

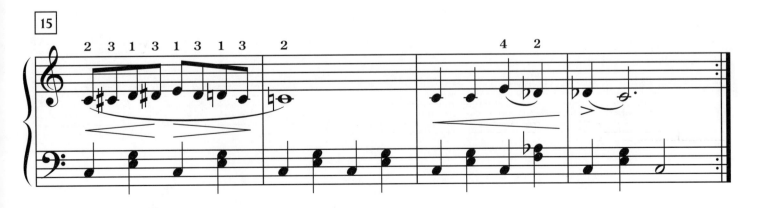

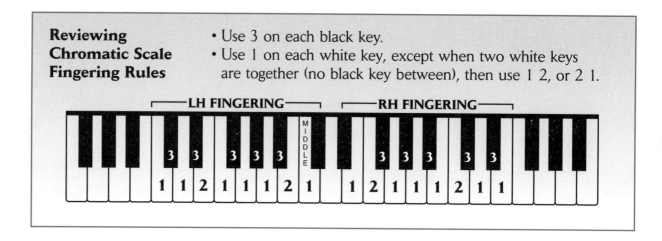

Reviewing Chromatic Scale Fingering Rules

- Use 3 on each black key.
- Use 1 on each white key, except when two white keys are together (no black key between), then use 1 2, or 2 1.

Write and Play Exercise

1. Write the chromatic scale, *ascending,* on the following *treble* staff. Use half notes. Use *sharps* to indicate black keys.

2. Write the chromatic scale, *descending,* on the following *bass* staff. Use half notes. Use *flats* to indicate black keys.

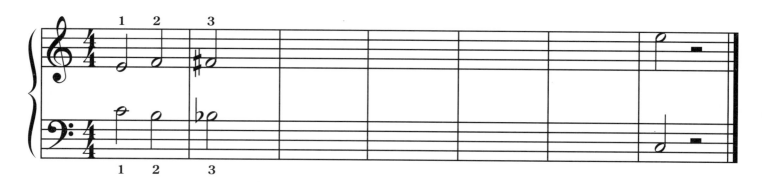

3. Write the chromatic scale, *descending,* on the following *treble* staff. Use half notes. Use *flats* to indicate black keys.

4. Write the chromatic scale, *ascending,* on the following *bass* staff. Use half notes. Use *sharps* to indicate black keys.

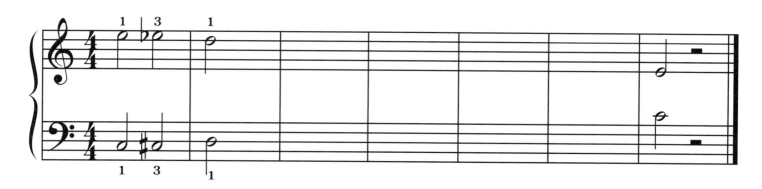

5. Add fingering to the exercises above, using the fingering rules on the top of this page.

6. Play everything on this page, hands separately and then together.

Circus March
(Entry of the Gladiators)

Fučik, a Bohemian bandmaster, also played the bassoon. He studied composition with Dvořák, and wrote many dances and marches for band.

Julius Fučik
(1872–1916)

Moderate march tempo

Eighth-Note Triplets

When three notes are grouped together with a figure "*3*" above or below the notes, the group is called a **triplet**.

> The three notes of an eighth-note triplet group equal one quarter note.
>
> When a piece contains triplets, count "trip-a-let" or "one & then" or any way suggested by your teacher.

Amazing Grace

John Newton, J. Carrell
and D. Clayton

Moderately slow

*****simile*** = same. This means *continue in the same manner.* In this case, continue to play triplets each time three eighth notes are joined with one beam.

Rhythm Exercise: Away from the Keyboard

Clap (or tap) the following rhythms, counting aloud.

Practice Exercise: Sight Reading

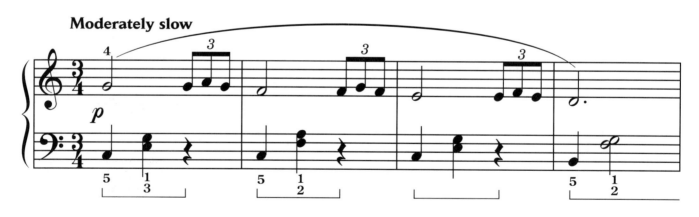

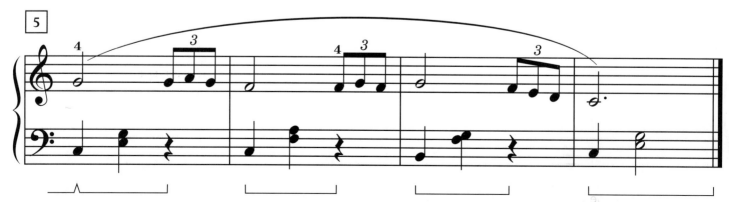

Movin' Along

*Eighth notes may be played unevenly, in long-short pairs.

D. C. al Fine

New Time Signature

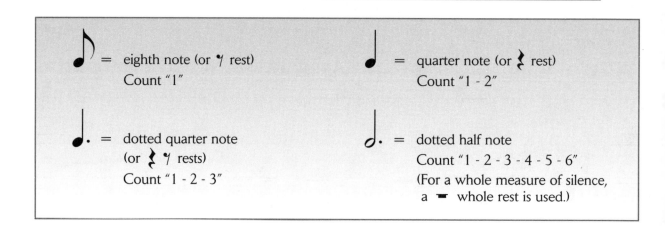

$\frac{6}{8}$ = **6** beats to each measure.

$\frac{6}{8}$ = **eighth note** ♪ gets **one** beat.

♪ = eighth note (or ⅞ rest)
Count "1"

♩ = quarter note (or 𝄽 rest)
Count "1 - 2"

♩. = dotted quarter note
(or 𝄽 ⅞ rests)
Count "1 - 2 - 3"

♩. = dotted half note
Count "1 - 2 - 3 - 4 - 5 - 6"
(For a whole measure of silence,
a ▬ whole rest is used.)

Rhythm Exercise: Away from the Keyboard

Clap (or tap) and following rhythms, counting aloud.

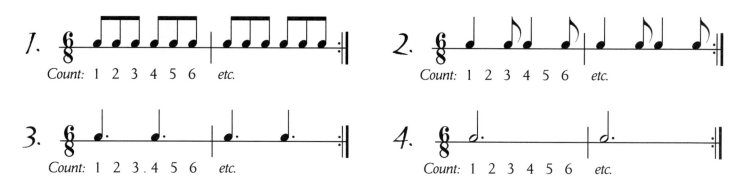

1. $\frac{6}{8}$
Count: 1 2 3 4 5 6   etc.

2. $\frac{6}{8}$
Count: 1 2 3 4 5 6   etc.

3. $\frac{6}{8}$
Count: 1 2 3 . 4 5 6   etc.

4. $\frac{6}{8}$
Count: 1 2 3 4 5 6   etc.

La Raspa

Lively
2nd time accelerando poco a poco al fine*

Latin Folk Tune

mf

* **Accelerando** means *gradually faster.* **Poco a poco** means *little by little.*
Accelerando poco a poco al fine means *gradually faster little by little to the end.*

D. C. al Fine

*__sf__ = __sforzando,__ Italian for "forcing." It means to play louder on one note or chord; in this case
it applies to the note above __sf__ and the chord below it.

Rhythm Exercise: Away from the Keyboard

Tap the following rhythms, counting aloud.

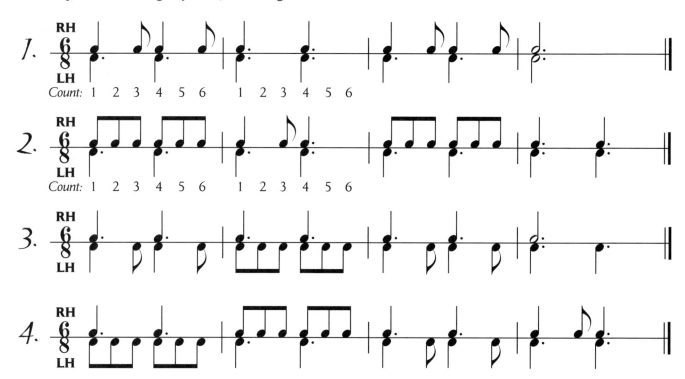

Practice Exercise: Sight Reading

Rhythm Exercise: Away from the Keyboard

Each of the following examples represents just *one measure* of music.

1. Write the time signature ($\frac{2}{4}$ $\frac{3}{4}$ $\frac{4}{4}$ or $\frac{6}{8}$) at the beginning of each line, as shown in the first example.

2. Count aloud and clap (or tap) once for each note.

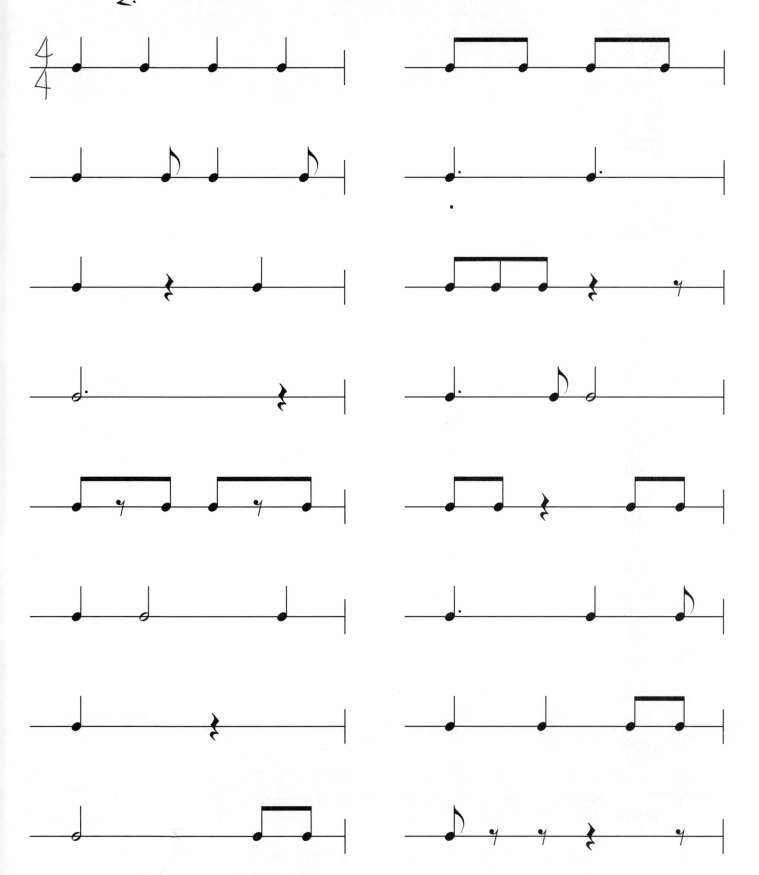

Tempo Indications

Tempo is an Italian word meaning "rate of speed."
In most music, tempo indications are given in Italian.

The measures from these familiar songs represent the
most widely-used tempos (tempi). Play and count
each excerpt.

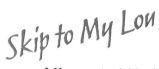
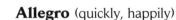

Allegro (quickly, happily)

Lavender's Blue

Andante (moving along, "walking speed")

Farewell to Thee
(Aloha Oe)

Queen L. K. Liliuokalani

Adagio (slowly)

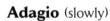
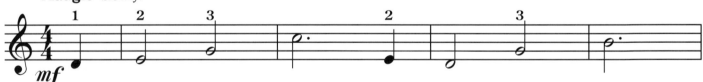

Largo (from "The New World")

Antonin Dvořák

Largo (very slowly)

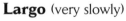

Lullaby

Johannes Brahms

Moderato (moderately)

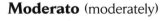

Moderato may be combined with the other words: **Allegro moderato** = moderately quick
Andante moderato = moderate walking speed

For He's a Jolly Good Fellow

Traditional

Mexican Hat Dance

Traditional

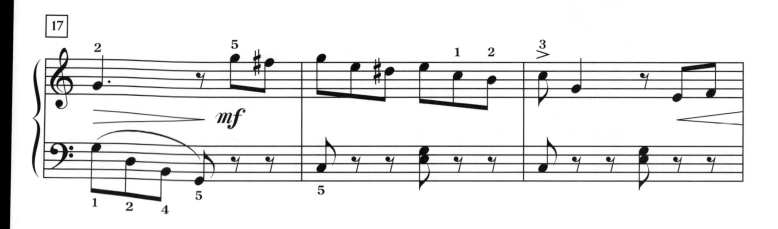

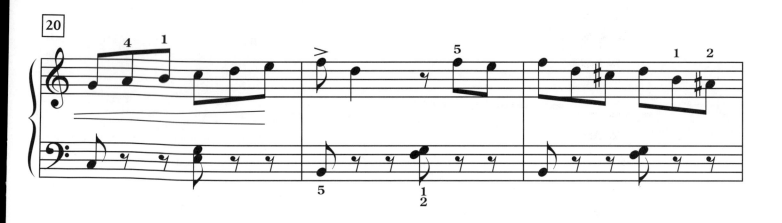

This piece is respectfully dedicated to the memory of world-renowned concert pianist, Vladimir Horowitz (1903–1989). Horowitz was a Russian by birth but became an American citizen in 1942. His recitals were sell-outs in concert halls throughout the world.

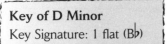

Key of D Minor
Key Signature: 1 flat (B♭)

Key of F Major (Relative of D Minor)

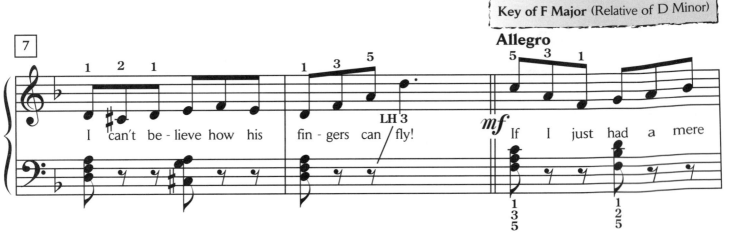

Scherzo. This word means *a musical jest or joke.* It is applied to light and playful pieces.

Key of D Minor

13

p I've a sus - pi - cion it's | more than am - bi - tion, it's | how man - y D. C. al

Note: Both hands now play in treble clef.

16

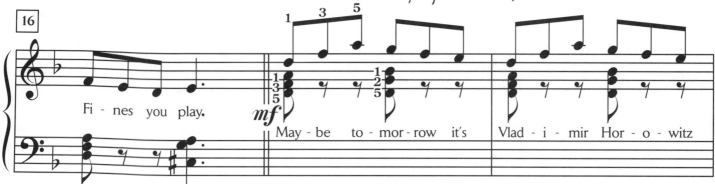

Fi - nes you play. | *mf* May - be to - mor - row it's | Vlad - i - mir Hor - o - witz

accelerando poco a poco al fine
Both hands 8va – – – – – – –

19

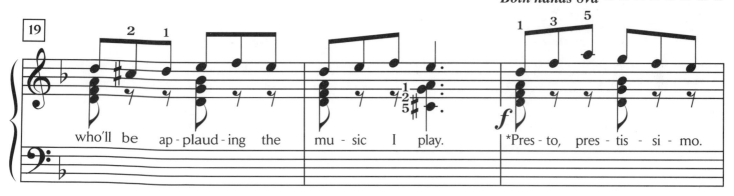

who'll be ap - plaud - ing the | mu - sic I play. | *f* *Pres - to, pres - tis - si - mo.

(Both hands 8va) –

22

**Brav - o, brav - is - si - mo! | I'm get - ting bet - ter and | bet - ter each day!

LH 3

*Presto.** Italian for "fast." This tempo mark means *faster than* **allegro.**

The word **prestissimo** means *very fast.* It usually means *as fast as possible.*

Bravo, bravissimo. These Italian words are often shouted by audiences of virtuoso performers. They can't be exactly translated, but they mean something like *"Marvelous,* very *marvelous!"*

Unit 10

The Key of E Minor

The Key of E Minor (Relative of G Major)

E minor is the relative minor of G major. Both keys have the same key signature (1 sharp, F#).

Remember: The relative minor begins on the *6th* tone of the major scale.

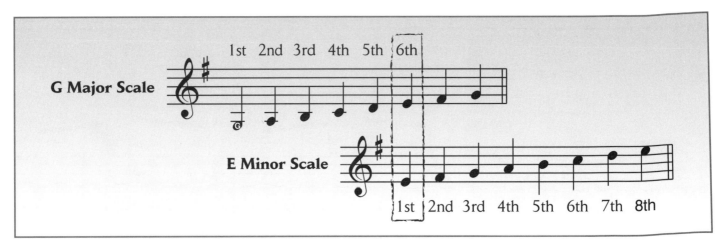

The minor scale shown above is the *natural minor* scale. Remember, the natural minor uses only notes that are found in the *relative major* scale.

The E Harmonic Minor Scale

In the *harmonic minor* scale, the 7th tone is raised ascending and descending.

The raised 7th in the key of E minor is D#. It is not included in the key signature, but is written as an accidental each time it occurs.

Practice the E harmonic minor scale hands separately. Begin slowly and gradually increase speed.

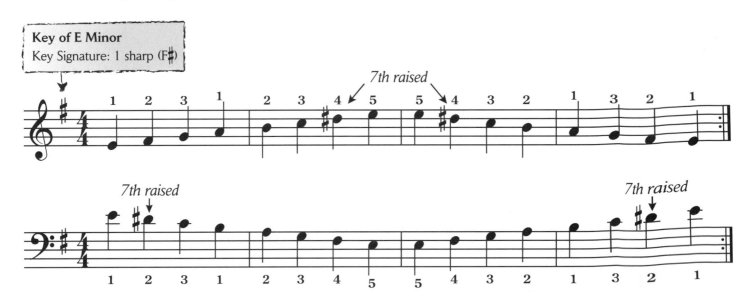

Important! After you have learned the E harmonic minor scale hands separately, you may play the hands together in contrary motion, by combining the two staffs above.

Practice Exercise: Sight Reading

1a.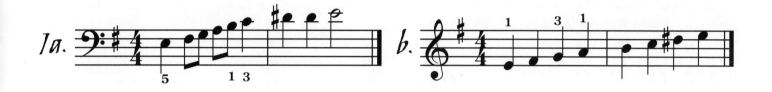

c. d.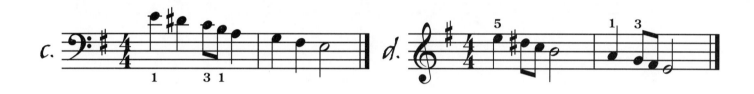

2a.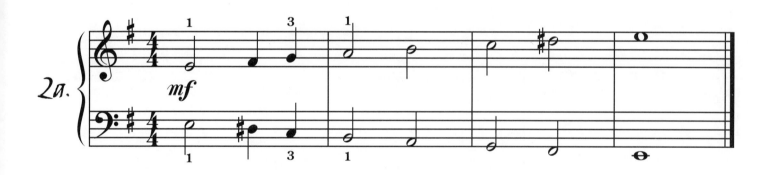

b.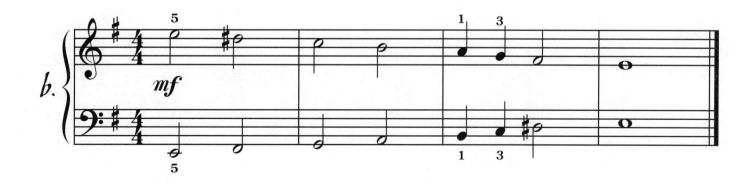

The House of the Rising Sun

Key of E Minor
Key Signature: 1 sharp (F♯)

Folk Song

Andante moderato
2nd time both hands 8va

Ped. simile = Continue to pedal in the same manner.

Write and Play Exercise

1. In the treble staff under the squares, write the notes of the E harmonic minor scale. Use whole notes. Add fingering above the notes and then play.

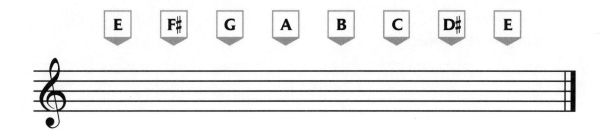

2. In the bass staff over the squares, write the notes of the E harmonic minor scale. Use whole notes. Add fingering below the notes and then play.

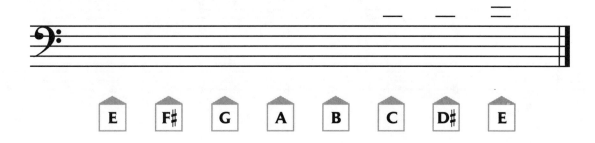

3. Write the name of each note in the square below it—then play and say the note names.

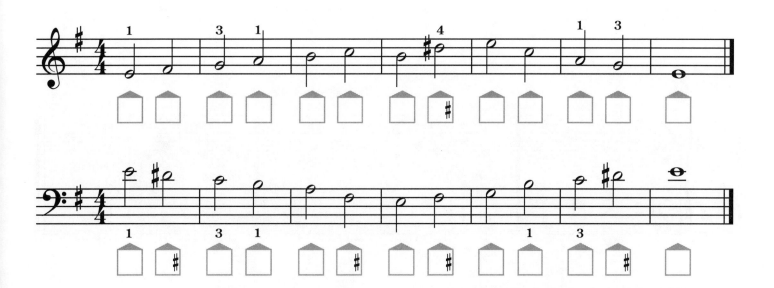

An Ancient Dance

Dances like this one were usually accompanied by a small drum called a tabor, and one or more small wind instruments.

17th Century French Dance

*__morendo__ = dying away. Get softer to the end.

Practice Exercise: Sight Reading

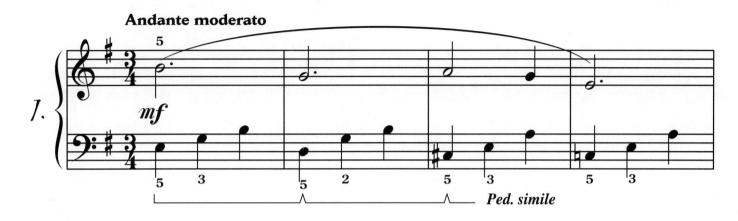

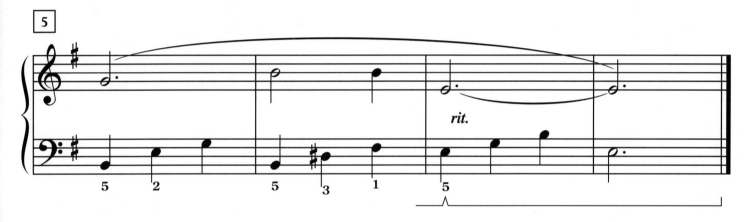

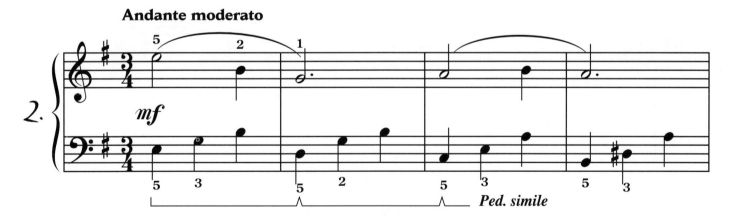

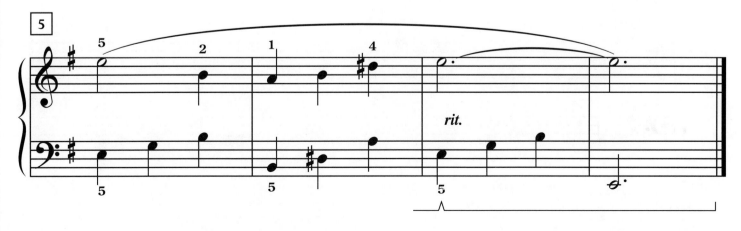

Primary Chords in E Minor

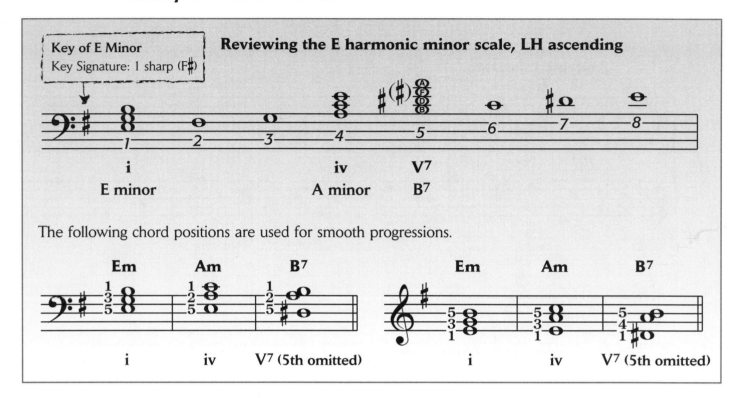

The following chord positions are used for smooth progressions.

E is the common tone between i and iv. B is the common tone between i and V^7.

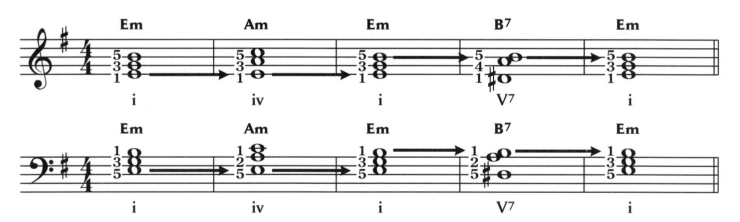

Write and Play Exercise

1. Rewrite the above progressions on the following staffs.

2. Add fingering. 3. Add arrows to show the common tones. 4. Play hands separately.

Em	Am	Em	B⁷	Em
i	iv	i	V⁷	i

Em	Am	Em	B⁷	Em
i	iv	i	V⁷	i

Sakura
(Cherry Blossoms)

Japanese Folk Song

Practice Exercise: Sight Reading

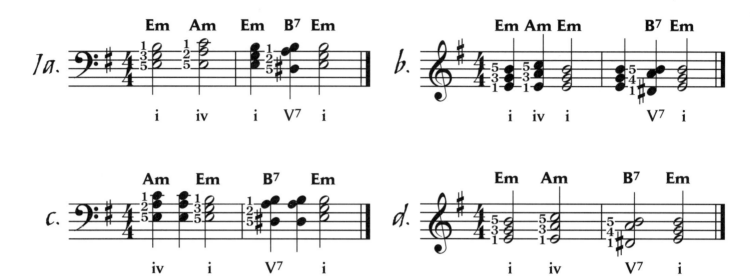

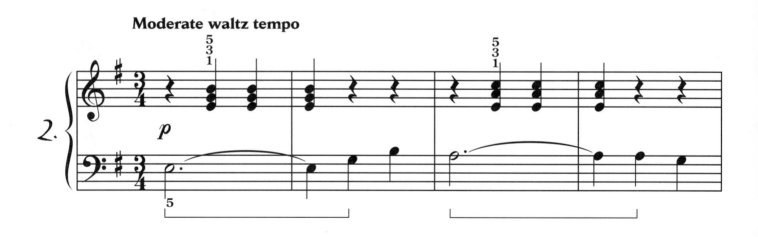

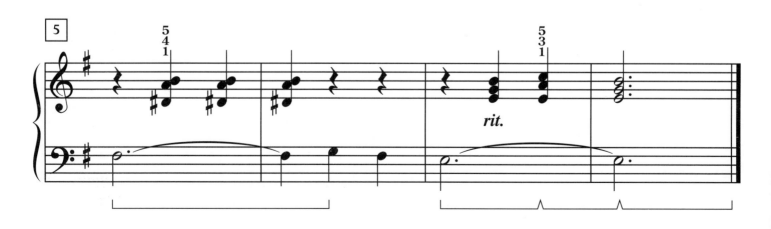

Written Exercise: Away from the Keyboard

1. In the squares above the staff, write the names of the notes in each chord.

2. On the staff, circle the root of each chord.

3. On the line below the staff, write the name of the chord (**i, iv** or **V⁷**).

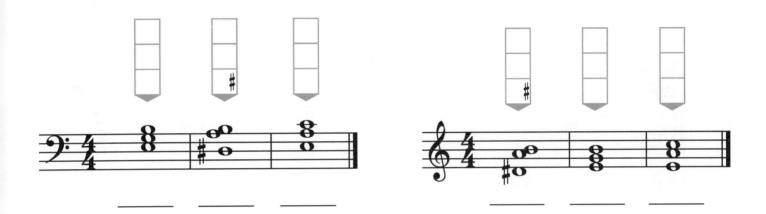

_____   _____   _____   _____   _____   _____

4. Draw a line from each box to its matching box in the adjacent column(s).

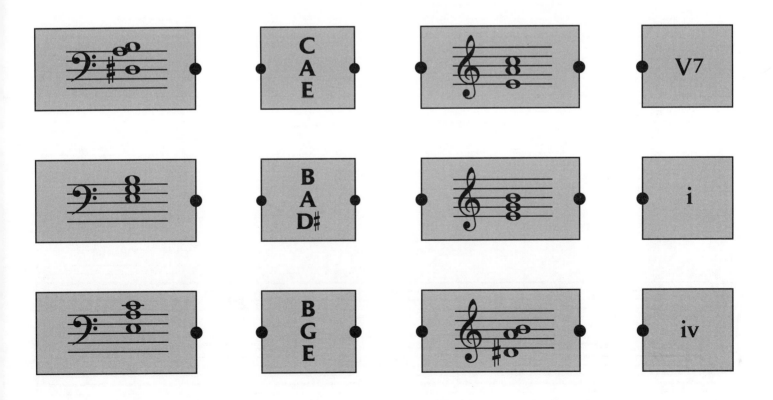

E Minor Progression with Broken Chords

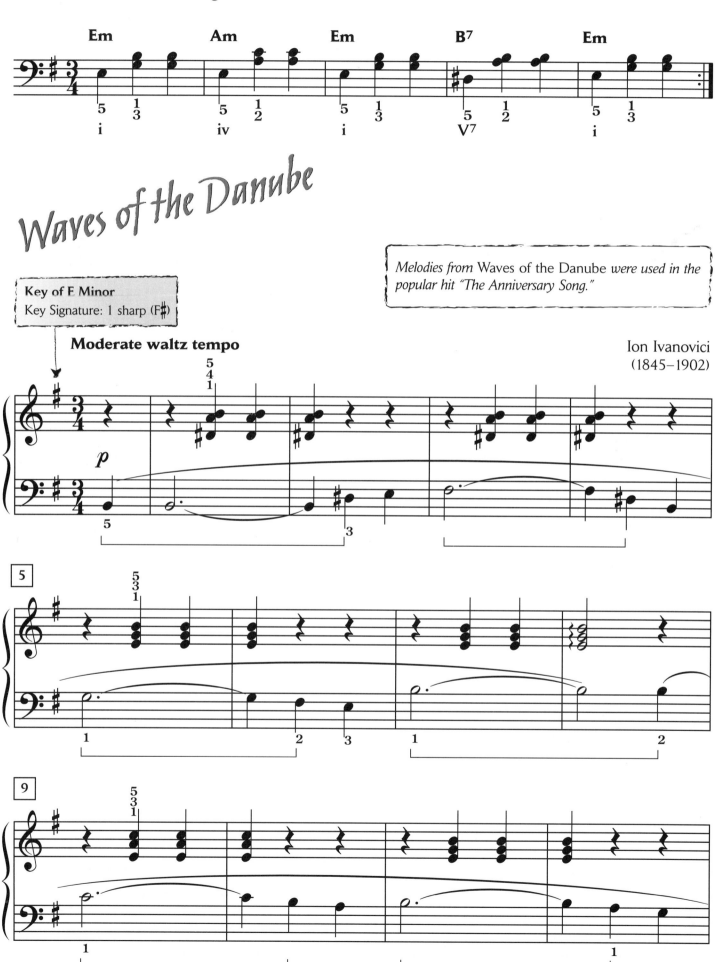

Waves of the Danube

Key of E Minor
Key Signature: 1 sharp (F#)

Melodies from Waves of the Danube *were used in the popular hit "The Anniversary Song."*

Moderate waltz tempo

Ion Ivanovici
(1845–1902)

The Erie Canal

*Dedicated to our friends at Vicks Litho, printers
of this book, who live near the Erie Canal.*

Traditional

Index

Glossary of Terms & Symbols

Includes all the new terms and symbols used in Book 2, and the page(s) on which they are introduced. Terms and symbols without page numbers were introduced in Book 1.

Accelerando	Gradually faster (p. 122).
Accent sign (>)	Play with special emphasis (p. 60).
Accidental	A sharp or flat that is not in the key signature. A natural sign is also an accidental (p. 72).
Adagio	A tempo indication meaning "slowly" (p. 126).
Allegro	A tempo indication meaning "quickly, happily" (p. 126).
Andante	A tempo indication meaning "moving along, walking speed" (p. 126).
Arpeggiated chords	When a wavy line appears before a chord, the chord is *arpeggiated* (broken or rolled) (p. 69).
A tempo	Resume original speed (p. 40).
Bar lines	Divide music into measures.
Bass clef sign (𝄢)	Helps identify notes below middle C; locates the F below the middle of the keyboard.
Block chord	When the notes of a chord are played together.
Blues	Music that follows a basic formula, that is, a standard chord progression (p. 25).
Broken chord	When the notes of a chord are played separately.
C major chord	C E G, G C E.
C position	LH 5 on the C below middle C; RH 1 on middle C.
Chord symbol	Used to identify chord names.
Chord	When three or more notes are played together.
Chord progression	When we change from one chord to another; a series of chords (p. 24).
Chromatic scale	A scale made up entirely of half steps. It goes up and down, using every key, black and white (p. 114).
Common time (𝄴)	Same as $\frac{4}{4}$ time (p. 96).
Contrary motion	Both hands play the same numbered fingers at the same time, while moving in opposite directions (p. 42).
Crescendo (⟨)	A dynamic sign that means to play gradually louder.
D. C. al Fine (Da Capo al Fine)	Means repeat from the beginning and play to the end (Fine).
D. S. 𝄋 al Fine (Dal Segno al Fine)	Means repeat from the sign (𝄋) and play to the end (Fine) (p. 52).
D⁷ chord	F♯ C D.
Damper pedal	The right pedal. When held down, any tone you sound will continue after you release the key.
Diminuendo (⟩)	A dynamic sign that means to play gradually softer.
Dotted half note (♩.)	Receives 3 counts in $\frac{3}{4}$ and $\frac{4}{4}$ time.
Dotted quarter note (♩.)	Equal to a quarter note tied to an eighth note.
Double bar line (‖)	Used at the end of a piece.
Dynamic signs	Tell how loud or soft to play.
Eighth notes (♫)	Two eighth notes are played in the time of one quarter note.
Eighth rest (𝄾)	Rest for the value of an eighth note (p. 70).
F major chord	F A C, C F A.
Fermata	Hold the note under the fermata longer than its value.
Fifth (5th)	When you skip three white keys. 5ths are written line-line or space-space.
Fine	End.
Finger substitution	Changing fingers on one note while holding the note down (p. 43, 81).
First and second endings	Play the notes under the first bracket the first time only; play the notes under the second bracket the second time (p. 47).

Flat sign (♭)	Play the next key to the left, whether black or white.
Forte (f)	Loud.
Fortissimo (ff)	Very loud (p. 15).
Fourth (4th)	When you skip two white keys. 4ths are written line-space or space-line.
G major chord	G B D.
G position	LH 5 on the G below middle C; RH 1 on the G above middle C.
G7 chord	B F G.
Grand staff	The bass staff and the treble staff joined together by a brace.
Half note (♩)	Receives 2 counts in $\frac{2}{4}$, $\frac{3}{4}$ and $\frac{4}{4}$ time.
Half rest (▬)	A sign of silence for the value of a half note.
Half step	The distance from any key to the very next key up or down, black or white, with no key between (p. 8).
Harmonic interval	The distance between two tones that are played together.
Harmonic minor	The minor scale in which the 7th tone is raised, ascending and descending (p. 72).
Incomplete measure	A measure at the beginning of a piece with fewer counts than indicated in the time signature.
Key	Music based on any particular scale is said to be in the key of that scale (p. 21).
Key note	The note on which a scale begins and ends (p. 13).
Key signature	The sharps or flats at the beginning of each staff of music that tell which notes are to be played sharp or flat, and also tell what key the piece is in (p. 21).
Largo	A tempo indication meaning "very slowly" (p. 126).
Legato	To smoothly connect two or more notes.
Leger line	A short line added above or below the staff to extend its range.
Line note	A note written on a line.
Loco	As written, not 8va (p. 54).
Major scale	Two tetrachords joined by a whole step (p. 13).
Major triad	A triad consisting of a root, major 3rd and perfect 5th (p. 76).
Measure	The area between two bar lines. Bar lines divide the music into measures of equal duration.
Melodic interval	The distance between two tones that are played separately.
Mezzo forte (mf)	Moderately loud.
Mezzo piano (mp)	Moderately soft (p. 40).
Middle C	The C nearest the middle of the piano.
Middle C position	Both thumbs are on middle C.
Minor triad	A triad consisting of a root, minor 3rd and perfect 5th (p. 76).
Moderato	A tempo indication meaning "moderately" (p. 126).
Morendo	Dying away. Get softer (p. 136).
Natural minor	The scale that uses only the notes of the relative major scale (p. 72).
Natural sign (♮)	Cancels a sharp (♯) or flat (♭) (p. 6).
N.C. (no chord)	Means to play no chord.
Notes	The symbols on the staff that indicate pitch and duration of tones.
Octave	Eight notes, or the interval of an 8th (when you skip 6 white keys). Octaves are written line-space or space-line.
Overlapping pedal	Changing pedal on a note or chord. Lift the pedal up and put it down again immediately (p. 80).
Perfect 5th	A 5th consisting of 7 half steps (p. 76).
Phrase	A musical thought or sentence.
Piano (p)	Soft.

Pianissimo (*pp*) — Very soft (p. 51).

Poco — little (p. 53).

Poco rit. — a little *ritardando* (p. 53).

Primary chords — The three most important chords of any key. They are built on the 1st, 4th and 5th notes of the scale (p. 24).

Quarter note (♩) — Receives 1 count in $\frac{2}{4}$, $\frac{3}{4}$ and $\frac{4}{4}$ time.

Quarter rest (𝄽) — A sign of silence for the value of a quarter note.

Repeat sign (:‖) — Repeat from the beginning.

Repeat signs (‖: :‖) — Repeat everything between the double bars (p. 63).

Repeated notes — Consecutive notes on the same line or space.

Relative major — See *relative minor* (p. 72).

Relative minor — Every major key has a relative minor key that has the same key signature. The relative minor begins on the 6th tone of the major scale (p. 72).

Rest — A sign of silence.

Rhythm — The combining of notes into patterns.

Ritardando (rit.) — Gradually slowing.

Root — The note on which a triad is built and from which the triad gets its name (p. 20).

Scherzo — Means "a musical jest or joke." It is applied to light and playful pieces (p. 130).

Second (2nd) — The distance from any white key to the next white key. 2nds are written line-space or space-line.

Seventh (7th) — When you skip five white keys. 7ths are written line-line or space-space.

Sforzando (*sf*) — Italian for "forcing." It means to play louder on one note or chord (p. 123).

Sharp sign (♯) — Play the next key to the right, whether black or white.

Simile — Continue in the same manner (pp. 14, 118, 134).

Sixth (6th) — When you skip four white keys. 6ths are written line-space or space-line.

Slur — A curved line over or under notes on different lines or spaces; means to play legato.

Space note — A note written in a space.

Staccato (♩ ♩) — The dot over or under a note. Play the note very short.

Staff — The five lines and four spaces on which music is written.

Skip (3rd) — Moving up or down from a line to the next line, or from a space to the next space.

Step (2nd) — Moving up or down from a line to the next space, or from a space to the next line.

Syncopated notes — Notes played between the main beats of the measure and held across the beat (pp. 6, 75, 83, 102, 106).

Tempo — Speed. Tells how fast or slow to play the music.

Tetrachord — A series of four notes having a pattern of whole step, whole step, half step (p. 12).

Third (3rd) — When you skip a white key. 3rds are written line-line or space-space.

Tied notes — When notes on the same line or space are joined with a curved line. The key is held down for the combined values of both notes.

Time signature ($\frac{4}{4}$, $\frac{3}{4}$, $\frac{2}{4}$, $\frac{6}{8}$) — Numbers that appear at the beginning of music. The top number tells the number of beats (counts) in each measure; the bottom number tells the kind of note that gets 1 beat (p. 122).

Treble clef sign (𝄞) — Helps identify notes above middle C; locates the G above the middle of the keyboard.

Triad — A three-note chord (p. 20).

Triplet — The three notes of an eighth-note triplet group equal one quarter note (p. 118).

Whole note (o) — Receives 4 counts in $\frac{4}{4}$ time.

Whole rest (▬) — A sign of silence for the value of a whole note or for one whole measure.

Whole step — Equal to two half steps. There is one key between (p. 9).